HIS COMFORT OF SILENCE

My Journey To Recovery
from Emotional Pain

3/26/15

Wayne,

The prayers & support from
my brothers & sisters in Christ helped
carry me through my journey.
Thank you!

Joyfully His,
Eriko

ERIKO N. VALK PH.D.
FOREWORD BY DIANN MILLS

D1445971

His Comfort of Silence: Journey to Recovery from Emotional Pain
Copyright © 2015 Eriko N. Valk Ph.D.
All rights reserved.
No part of this book may be reproduced, stored in a retrieval system, or transmit-
ted in any form by any means—electronic, mechanical, photocopying, recording, or
otherwise—except for brief quotations in printed reviews, without prior permis-
sion in writing from the author. Requests for permission should be submitted to
Dr.V@erikovalk.com
Scripture quotations are taken from THE HOLY BIBLE, NEW INTERNATIONAL
VERSION®, NIV® Copyright © 1973, 1978, 1984, 2011-2015, by Biblica, Inc.®,
Used by permission. All rights reserved worldwide.
ISBN: 1502523450
ISBN 13: 9781502523457
Library of Congress Control Number: 2014917579
CreateSpace Independent Publishing Platform
North Charleston, South Carolina

In Loving Memory of Patsy Ward Burk
11/20/1936–11/09/2013

In Honor of My Family

For His Glory

TABLE OF CONTENTS

FOREWORD

Dr. ERIKO VALK, fondly referred to as Dr. V, has been a dear friend of mine for many years. We've shared our mountains and valleys and laughed at what the world tosses our way. But what impresses me most about Eriko is this: She remains a survivor. Once you've read *His Comfort of Silence*, you will agree only God could have touched her life and created the woman of God she is today.

Eriko has always impressed me with her compassion for hurting people, not simply as a tug on her heart, but to reach out and help others find peace and purpose in their lives.

She experienced the chains of addiction, overwhelming despair, and incredible loneliness known only by those who suffer without hope. Her unique ministry surfaced from overcoming her own life challenges and personal pain through her faith in Jesus Christ, the great Healer.

Transparency, love, and knowledge of the human heart and mind are reflected throughout the following pages. Eriko shares her life story through raw footage of how she slipped into the depths of anguish and rose to victory. God was with her all the way, holding her hand when she wanted to let go, loving her when she felt unlovable, and nurturing her as only a true Father can. And He will do that for you.

Walk with my friend on her journey to healing. From grief to celebration, Dr. Eriko Valk has helped hundreds of people embrace life. Read her story and find healing joy in the grace of God.

You will be blessed.

DiAnn Mills, Award-winning Author
www.diannmills.com

"Eriko masterfully weaves a firsthand account of deep personal wounds with solid scriptural ointment into a narrative that offers a path for healing for those struggling with damaging pasts."

Mark Lanier
Author, Biblical Teacher, and Lawyer

"*His Comfort of Silence* is a timely story of hope. It is a poignant biography of one woman's courageous path of healing and comfort through severe abandonment, affliction, and abuse. Her inspiring journey of transformation through intense pain offers a path for others to find this same healing and comfort no matter what circumstances they find themselves in. In a day of medical diagnoses, medication, and anesthetizing of pain, *His Comfort of Silence* offers a liberating path for the hopeless to find this same hope, the afflicted to find comfort, the addicted to find healing, and for those who feel alone to find this same personal relationship with the One who will never leave or forsake them, the Lord Jesus Christ.

Dr. Eriko Valk is a living testimony of God's transformative power. Her life story is poured out in detail for God's glory, so that through her story, His story brings comfort, hope, transformation, and peace to other overcomers."

Sandy Bond, MA
Licensed Professional Counselor

"Having been Eriko's pastor and friend for several years, I've always been impressed with her faith and determination. Nothing surprises me about her accomplishments, because while she may not be large in stature, she knows and listens to a big God. And He has done incredible things through her. I believe this story will encourage anyone who feels life is difficult and unfair because it will show them that when you listen to God, He brings healing to your soul. This story is a wonderful testimony of the miracle of God's grace."

Bryan Donahoo
Pastor
Graceview Baptist Church

"I have only known the adult Eriko—the kind, gentle, compassionate Eriko. Her book helps me to understand where she gets her passion to help the brokenhearted. We all deal with conflicts and challenges each day, and whether that is addiction, abuse, or physical trials, I think Eriko's words offer encouragement and direction toward the ultimate healing relationship with God."

Pamela E. Harris, PhD
President
TrueNorth Compliance, Inc.

"In *His Comfort of Silence*, Dr. Eriko N. Valk shares her gripping story of abuse and deafness, the descent into alcoholism, and the light that led her on the path to freedom. When you reach the end of one page, you will find yourself eager to turn it, and find out what happens on the next page. Little by little, the words shared will awaken in you hope and the miraculous wonder of a life transformed.

While reading Eriko's journey of recovery, you will come to know the compassion, love, and mercy of God—the God of grace and forgiveness. The truth and wisdom contained in *His Comfort of Silence* will set you free, and guide you on your own journey of healing and restoration. Whether you are completely broken or have already experienced a level of healing, this book will open your eyes even more to the only thing—the only One—who can mend life's deepest wounds.

Eriko's testimony will inspire you to overcome your own limitations, negative experiences, and seemingly impossible odds to fulfill God's unique plan for your life. You will soon see this plan is greater than you or anyone else ever imagined. Let the light that shines through the pages of *His Comfort of Silence* lead you along your own liberty path—a path where every hurt is redeemed and repurposed for your good, the good of others, and God's glory. What incredible comfort you will experience when the lies that have plagued you are finally silenced!"

Michelle Flippin
Author and Speaker
Houston, Texas

"I was honored to profile Eriko as one of our Jefferson Award recipients in 2009. She continues her efforts to help others navigate through troubled pasts to chart a more promising future. This time, she bravely digs into the deep crevices of her own vessel and shows how one can mend structural holes and set sail. Bravo, Eriko!"

Dominique Sachse
Emmy®-winning News Anchor and Reporter
KPRC Local 2
Houston, Texas

ACKNOWLEDGMENTS

MAY GOD BESTOW His blessings and favor upon the following individuals and groups who helped me share my story through *His Comfort of Silence:*

DiAnn Mills, Christy Award-winning author, and Michelle Flippin, an inspirational speaker and author, both of whom asked probing questions, provided wisdom to get my manuscript on the right track, and gently guided me through the editing process,

My church and my recovery families, who are always there for me and have taught me the value of serving others,

Our volunteers, counselors, and staff of Liberty Path, Inc., who have lifted me up in prayer throughout this endeavor, and

My husband and children, who encourage, inspire, and love me—just as I am.

INTRODUCTION

I DIDN'T WAKE up one morning and say, "Gee, I think I'll be an alcoholic when I grow up." In fact, I woke up many mornings wishing I wasn't.

If you have difficulty understanding why God has allowed you to abuse alcohol or prescription drugs, or why He has allowed you to experience turmoil, abuse, and other struggles, I'm thankful you are reading this.

This is my story of healing and recovery from abuse, addiction, alcoholism, and deafness. I share my pain and struggles as well as my triumphs with a good sprinkle of humor. You will see how God turned everything that Satan meant for my harm into good for me and my family, and also for the clients now served at our Christian-based counseling center, Liberty Path, Inc., which I founded in 2004.

My story is written with a prayer that it offers you hope, healing, recovery, and restoration. You are not alone. God *does* have a plan for you, my friend.

1

*"'For I know the plans I have for you,' declares
the Lord, 'plans to prosper you and not to harm
you, plans to give you hope and a future.'"*
JEREMIAH 29:11

MY MOTHER COULD have chosen not to give birth to me, and there were many days, months, and even years I wished I were never born. I know she loved me, because she ultimately made the biggest sacrifice of all for me.

By the time I was four years old, in 1954, I already had some good memories, some not-so-good.

A Special Treat
Post World War II, the city of Otsu, Japan, was a little fishing village not far from Kyoto. That's where my mother, Matsue (pronounced *Maht-sue-eh*), gave birth to me, an illegitimate child. We didn't have very much. We lived in a one-room house with no running water or indoor plumbing. However, our house was on prime real estate, right along the water's edge of Lake Biwa and within walking distance to an army base.

On days when extra money was available, Matsue and I would venture into the big city of Kyoto. Matsue would say, "Let's catch the bus and ride into town! We will have us a grand time, just you and me." Of course, all of this was spoken in Japanese, my native language.

In Kyoto, we would be treated to a community bath with hot water. What a special treat that was. In Otsu, we would bathe in a mountain stream that ran behind our house. The water was ice cold, even during the warmer summer months because the water flowed from a mountain nearby.

After our hot bath, we would sit in a shop and eat, drink, laugh, and talk. "Shall we go window-shopping? What shall we buy?" Matsue would ask. "I know: Let's go to the theater first!" Off we would go to the Kabuki theater, where all actors are male, followed by a window-shopping stroll. We would look at all the beautiful things displayed in the windows. We knew we would never own those beautiful clothes, fashionable shoes, dresses, and toys, but it was still fun to dream.

On one of the last outings Matsue and I had together, she allowed me to take a sip of her saké, a Japanese rice wine often served warm. I immediately felt the inside-out warm glow—it was unforgettable. Even after leaving the sushi shop, I remember smiling, laughing, and being giddy. My cheeks were glowing, and my behavior made Matsue laugh. Seeing Matsue laugh was very rare. She was so sad most of the time. The years after World War II were a difficult time to be an unwed mother in Japan with a child who looked very American.

"Oh, you are so funny, my child! You really know how to make my heart smile," Matsue said as she glowed with joy. The alcohol let me be free and giddy. It felt good to know my silly behavior put a smile on her face and lifted her spirits. I felt somehow responsible for her happiness. From that day forward, I chased those warm, carefree emotions. Well, at least until alcohol quit being my friend.

Fishing

Not all my early memories were pleasant. One day, Matsue said, "I have the perfect game we can play. Let's go outside and take a boat ride. It will be so much fun!" In our fishing community, rowboats were a familiar site along the shore's edge.

My mother placed me in a small rowboat leaning on a log not far from our house. Strangely, Matsue did not come in the rowboat with me. Instead, she pushed the rowboat, and I started drifting away.

I looked around me and saw I was alone. My mother was no longer standing on the beach. She had disappeared. Where did she go? What was happening? There was no land, no trees, and no other boats. Nothingness was engulfing me in solitude.

"Can anyone hear me? Do you see me? I'm all alone in this boat. I don't know how to swim, and there's not even a paddle for me to use. Please...Come and get me, Mother!"

Matsue didn't answer. She couldn't hear my desperate cry because she was gone. She was nowhere to be seen. Alone in the middle of the lake, I became hungry, thirsty, and, most of all, frightened.

The orange sun dipped into the water as it started to rest for the day, encasing the lake with a golden hue. I continued to cry. Soon, I was depleted of energy, and my tears ran dry. The eerie darkness began to swallow me up.

I lay down and looked for the moon. "Mr. Moon, you have to help me. You have to give me light." Sure enough, Mr. Moon did exactly that. I didn't even know about God yet, but God was watching over me, providing light where none existed.

The silhouette of another boat took form, and the shadow began to draw nearer and nearer to me. The stench from the fishermen's catch of the day reached me before their boat did. Their boat was much larger than the little rowboat that captured me adrift. The two men in the boat, with their supply of fishnets and their abundant catch, were now clearly visible. They held lanterns up to their faces, casting an ominous glow. One spoke.

"Don't worry, little girl. We are here to help you. How did you get here?" The man tied our two boats together and then took me into their boat. For some reason, I was not afraid. After all, Mr. Moon gave light, and Mr. Moon brought these fishermen to help me, right? The fishermen gave me food and drink while providing soothing words to chase away my fears as they started to navigate toward the shore. In between sobs, I relayed the story to the fishermen of the game Matsue and I had played.

"Don't cry, little one. You are safe. You will see your mother soon."

We slowly made our way toward land. After what seemed like hours, we anchored and got off the boat. My mother appeared from nowhere, and she was waving her arms frantically.

"Here you go, little girl. You are safe now." The fishermen had found my mother. We all shed many tears.

"*Okasan* (Mother), why didn't you come for me? Why did you push the boat away and not get in? There were no paddles, and I can't swim! I was so afraid."

"Hush, my child. Everything is going to be all right." Matsue cried big tears. Perhaps she shed tears because she was happy I was found and returned safely to her. Perhaps disappointment caused her tears. I'll never know. I was crying too. My tears were mingled with relief and confusion. We both cried and cried what seemed to be an endless river of tears until we were both cried out.

> "*Record my misery; list my tears on your*
> *scroll; Are they not in your record?*"
> PSALM 56:8

After my mother put dry clothes on me, she unbraided my long, brown hair and used her brush to get the tangles out. She brushed my hair with gentle strokes while speaking soothing words. Her voice comforted me, and eventually I drifted off to sleep.

After the experience of my very first boat ride, I never wanted to set foot in a boat again. My fears of water, drowning, and being eaten by fish tormented me for many, many years. But God in His mercy has provided healing from those fears.

"Let's go fishing!" How I love to hear those words being spoken. My husband, Randall, and I spend our weekends in Freeport, Texas. We go fishing offshore with friends or just with each other.

What a miracle it is I am no longer afraid of getting in a boat. Too many years of my life were spent living in fear of being on the water. Too many years were spent living in fear of failing. Fear of the opposite sex. Fear of, well, everything!

Safe to Approach

One of the ways Matsue earned money to provide for me was by cleaning wealthy people's homes along the water's edge. She did not have a husband who provided for her, nor did she have any skills other than offering her services to others.

I would often sit outside by the lake and let my fantasies roam. I made up stories in my mind about the people who lived in those mansions. I know today they really weren't mansions at all; they were modest homes much bigger than our own. The world looks different to a young child, especially a curious child, and I was very curious.

One large home drew my attention, perhaps because it was the closest and within walking distance along the lakeshore. Any home larger than our one-room shack would have seemed extremely large, and this indeed looked like a mansion to me! In this "mansion" lived two boys who were probably around the ages of fourteen and sixteen. I was probably around four.

Hunger was often a big part of my life. That's not to say I went without a meal. We always had rice and fish, although neither was available to us in abundance. Because we lived on the lake, fishermen would come by occasionally to barter their fish for Matsue's "services."

One day, I finally had the courage to go next door to the "big" house. My mother was busy providing services to visitors, and I was not allowed in our house until she said it was okay. The curiosity of how others lived, what went on in that big house, how it looked on the inside (how many rooms, etc.) tempted me. I just had to go on this adventure.

The two boys were sitting outside on their front porch, smoking cigarettes, and eating. They had so much food! They had sushi, soup, ginger, and all the foods common to other Japanese households in abundance. It was like a restaurant. I was in awe, and I was hungry.

Because the boys were laughing and joking, I thought it was safe to approach them, but I was wrong. The boys eyed me with curiosity as I approached, and they gestured for me to come closer. I had trouble hearing and understanding what they were saying. How was I to know I was deaf in my left ear? I had never seen a doctor for anything.

"Little girl, we won't hurt you. Would you like to eat? We have plenty of food, and we will give you saké, too!" The boys offered me a plate of sushi, and then mockingly jerked it away, laughing with each other as I reached for the plate. I was just not fast enough or tall enough.

What transpired was a bribe of sorts: their plates of food in exchange for allowing them to touch me. "Don't worry. We are not going to hurt you. We just want to know what you feel like. It's not wrong. We are just curious boys."

The smaller of the boys said I didn't have to do anything. "Just let us touch, and we'll give you all the food and saké you want." They promised not to hurt me and said it would be our secret.

The desire for a full plate of delicacies was too much for me to resist. The only time Matsue and I ate sushi was when we went into Kyoto, and that was only if we had extra money, which was rare. This desire to have sushi and saké surpassed the apprehension growing within me. After all, Matsue had allowed her night visitors to touch me, so this had to be okay. The only difference was she wasn't here this time.

The boys took me to a room in their big house. You can use your imagination about what two adolescent boys would do in a situation like this and you'd be pretty accurate. The two boys immediately stopped and apologized when I started to cry. They also kept up their end of the deal. I got my plate of sushi to eat and saké to drink. The saké suppressed my emotions of shame.

My absolute loathing of sushi took root that day. It took me many decades to even be able to look at sushi without wanting to vomit. I never told my mother or anyone else about this little bartering occasion. I felt shame, embarrassment, and guilt. How could I have made such a trade? I was a young child, but I knew what I had allowed the boys to do. I felt dirty on the inside. The whole situation felt wrong.

Looking back over the years, I have often wondered what would have happened if I hadn't agreed to the exchange? Would those two teens have taken me by force? Would my life have turned out differently?

I give God thanks for watching over me and taking care of all the "what if's" in my life. He is the only one who knows not only of my past, my present, and my future, but He also knows all the "what if's" and He protects me. He protects me from my fears and from all the "what if's" life can bring.

"Give thanks in all circumstances;
for this is God's will for you in Christ Jesus."
FIRST THESSALONIANS 5:18

What's for Dinner?

"Where do you want to go eat?" my husband, Randall, will ask when he needs a break from meal preparation. (I rarely cook.) Often, my choice is to eat at any restaurant that offers sushi. Because of God's healing grace, I look forward to eating sushi. His miracles are abundant. What if I had chosen not to forgive those curious boys who lived in that mansion? What if I had not been able to forgive myself?

Tall and Blond

Other than cleaning the big house next door, Matsue did not "work" outside the home. She provided services in exchange for badly needed medical supplies, food, and money. Remember, this was post-World War II. Times were difficult for many Japanese citizens.

Matsue would say cheerfully, *"Eriko-san,* I will do everything I can to provide for you. Don't worry, my child. I will keep you with me for as long as I can." I sure didn't know what the last part of that sentence meant. For as long as she can? What does a young child know of these things? I am grateful today for all the sacrifices Matsue made for me during the years I lived with her. But trust me, for over half my life I loathed her and blamed her for my existence.

I did not know Matsue and I did not have a "normal" Japanese family. Or, maybe it was normal. I loved my mother, and I believed she loved me, too.

As we only had one room, I saw it all. I saw the late-afternoon and night visitors who came to be with her. In addition, sometimes I had to permit her guests to sleep with me. They would give me saké to drink so I would fall asleep. I wanted to be a good daughter and not disappoint her. After all, I was responsible for her happiness, right? *"Okasan,* I want to be a good girl. I want to make you happy. Please don't cry!" The need to please my mother was great. I wanted her to be happy.

None of her visitors ever hurt me, nor did they do the unspeakable as far as I know.

There was one visitor who only came in the light of day and did not stay overnight. He was very tall. (Anyone taller than my mother, who seemed larger than life herself, was very tall). He always wore a white uniform—not green like the others who visited. He wore a hat (part of his uniform), and when he took it off, I could see his thick, blond hair.

The tall man would talk to me. "How are you, *Eriko-san*? Did you have fun today?" He frequently brought me beautiful ribbons of all colors for my long, brown hair. "I hope you like these ribbons. I picked them out especially for you to go with your long, brown hair." He also brought Matsue and I sweets and chocolates—such rare treats for those of us who were struggling. In addition, he brought medical supplies.

The tall, blond stranger gave me a ragdoll I still have today. I had never owned a doll, so I didn't know what to call her. The tall, blond stranger suggested I name her "Mary," so I did. Mary used to cry when she was tipped over. Today, she is broken and silent and still loved very much.

As an adult, I have wondered if that tall, blond visitor was my father. Letters I received from Matsue many years later indicate my father was a physician in the military and was of Dutch descent. His name was Erik. Was that the tall, blond stranger? I'll never know for certain, but I believe he was indeed my father.

It used to be so important to me—a matter of life and death—to know who my birth father is for certain. Today, I know whoever my earthly father is, whether he was the tall, blond stranger or not, I have a Father who will never leave me. Ever.

"A father to the fatherless, a defender of widows,
is God in His holy dwelling."
PSALM 68:5

2

New Parents

OUR HOME ON Lake Biwa, Otsu, was within walking distance of an army base. This is where Matsue met my future parents-to-be: Jesse, a dark-skinned soldier, and his wife, Helen.

Sometime during the year 1955, I recall Matsue standing in front of our shack, waving at me. I sat inside a big, green car with the two strangers. Helen said, "We are your new parents. You can't live like this. You will have a new home, and soon we will go to America."

"*No!* I don't need new parents. I don't need a new mommy or a daddy. My mommy and I get along just fine. She takes care of me and loves me!" I screamed from the backseat as I waved, cried, and tried to understand. Matsue continued to shrink until the fog finally enveloped her. I continued to cry and wail. "I want Mommy! Please, please take me back home!"

I did not understand Matsue and I, mother and child, would no longer be together. I did not understand these two strangers in the car with me were going to be my new parents. I did not understand anything at all.

What a dreadful child I must be! My mother doesn't want me anymore! My body shook as I sobbed and screamed hysterically. I cried out, "What is going on?" This was the first time I had ever been in a car. Matsue and I had always walked or ridden the bus. It was, however, the second time Matsue disappeared from my sight.

Helen, a fair-skinned woman, was half French and half Japanese, so she was able to speak to me in Japanese, my native language. "*Eriko-san*, you cannot live with that woman any longer. You are getting a better life! You will see; just wait. And for God's sake, stop that crying. There's nothing to cry about!"

I guess she was trying to explain things to me, but I was so hysterical, I was unable to comprehend what she was trying to say. Why did I need a new mother? I never had a father, so why do I need one now? Matsue and I were doing just fine!

After that, two big questions plagued me for most of my life: Had I been such a terrible child my own mother didn't want me anymore? What was wrong with me? These questions remained unanswered until I was well into adulthood. The answers came when God prepared me to hear Him instead of the voices in my head.

"Call to me and I will answer you and tell you great and Unsearchable things you do not know."
JEREMIAH 33:3

My House

For the first few months, I tried to run away from Helen and Jesse's house. I wanted to be with my mother. I knew the bus routes pretty well, and even as a child, I was able to find my way home via the bus. After I found my way back to Matsue's home, the outhouse became my secret hiding place. It smelled nasty. When Helen and Jesse drove over and found me in my hiding place, I had to return with them to their house. "Tell me why I can't live with my mother!" I cried out. "I'll be good. Just let me go home!" To be ripped away from the only person I loved and knew as my mother hurt and confused me. I didn't understand what was going on.

On one of my runaway excursions, it became dark by the time I was able to catch the bus to go back home. The bus driver dropped me off at my stop, which was a good walking distance from my house on the lake. He cautioned, "Be careful, little one. It's dark. Are you sure you know where you're going?"

I lied and said, "Of course! I know the way!"

There was no one available to ask for directions, and the roads did not have streetlights. God was so merciful in watching over me even then. Once again, there was a brilliant full moon and I asked, "Mr. Moon, please help me find my house." I followed the direction of the moonlight, and it led me to the right road and on to my house.

To this day, I marvel at God's saving grace. He provided light when darkness surrounded me. He showed me the right path to take.

"God made two great lights—the greater light to govern the day and the lessor light to govern the night. He also made the stars."
GENESIS 1:16

God Only Knows

When Jesse was finally transferred from Japan to California, I could no longer find my way back to my mother's outhouse. I could no longer follow the moon back home.

After many years of struggling with anger and feelings of abandonment and pain, I saw what a tremendous sacrifice Matsue made. As a single mother, she did the best she could, and she wanted me to have a better life than the one before me in Japan. As a post-World War II baby, I was shunned in the little Japanese fishing village of Otsu for two reasons: I was an American soldier's baby, and I looked very American in a very Japanese community. I didn't know it at the time but later discovered Matsue's family completely disowned her because she chose to give me life, to keep me, and raise me. She had brought shame to her wealthy relatives by giving birth to an illegitimate American child. Matsue was severed from all family relationships.

For many years, I thought I was "bad." I believed lies that I was too ugly and unwanted. I thought it was all about me. I failed to see what a tremendous sacrifice Matsue made: giving up her only child for adoption even if it meant providing opportunities for me in a faraway country called America.

I have no way of knowing what my life would have been like had I stayed in Japan. God is the only one who knows. God has continued to be faithful and continues to take care of all the "what if's" in my life.

On many occasions, I have reflected on the pain God must have endured when He gave up His only begotten Son on the cross, so you and I might have forgiveness of sins and eternal life with Him.

Help! I'm Falling!

I laugh out loud when I recall some of the "firsts" I experienced after the adoption. For example, we all know how to sit on a toilet, right? Well, I had never seen a commode before. Remember the outhouse? I was used to squatting when nature called. Potty training me truly tested Helen's patience. She would say, "Just sit on it! Nothing will happen to you, you stupid child!" Her words didn't help my fears at all. When I had to sit on a commode for the first time, I was so afraid I would fall in. It took several months, during which many words of shame were hurled at me, before I could sit on a toilet without the fear of falling in and getting caught up in the swirl.

I also feared getting on escalators. I was astonished to watch people reach another level of a building without having to move their feet—what a scary magic trick! I would say, "Helen, everyone will get their feet chewed up and spit out by those big, shiny steel teeth! We have to tell them to stop!" Helen and Jesse got tired of using the stairs to go to another level. I refused with a vengeance to go on escalators. Gradually, after several whimpering attempts, I mastered the art of riding on an escalator. Helen and Jesse no longer had to walk to different levels.

Today, many opportunities exist for me to ride an escalator, whether in a shopping mall or at the airport. I chuckle silently and sometimes out loud, too, with joy and a sense of accomplishment. It's a small thing, but God wants us to take delight in the simple joys of life that He gives us each day.

Were you ever afraid of falling off your bed? I was! It took me about a year to feel safe in bed. Growing up, I slept on the floor as did my mother. In Japan, our beds were mats (called *tatamis*) we rolled out on the floor in a corner of our one-room shack. The floor was hard, and I did not have to worry about falling off. I was comfortable and felt safe. Except for when my mother was "working."

Today, I don't have any qualms about sleeping on a bed. I no longer have the fear of falling off a bed. Many bed manufacturers give you a choice to select the firmness of the mattress. My husband and I recently chose to purchase a bed that allows each half to be at different levels of firmness. My half is close to being as hard as the floor. Imagine that!

Most of us in our American culture know how to use a fork. As a young child, chopsticks were the only utensil I used. Helen and Jesse would get so angry and frustrated with me. "Eat like an American! After all, you're in America now." I just didn't understand. Why would people want to stab their food, especially peas? Weren't they afraid of poking the inside of their mouths? How strange! Nonetheless, I had to fit in. So, with much practice, I also mastered the art of eating with American utensils. My peas don't fall off the fork, and I rarely think about having to stab my food. Eating out at an Asian restaurant gives me an opportunity to use chopsticks, which still feel natural and comfortable.

My Citizenship

"Who was the first president of the United States?" the stern judge asked me as I stood before him in the overcrowded courtroom.

"Why, it was George Washington!" I answered, with a big grin on my face. After all the hours of studying for this very important exam, the judge only asked me this one question. He then asked me to recite the *Pledge of Allegiance*, which I had memorized.

> *"But our citizenship is in heaven. And we eagerly await a Savior from there, the Lord Jesus Christ, who will transform our lowly bodies so that they will be like His glorious body."*
> PHILIPPIANS 3:20–21

Shortly after some questions to others in the courtroom, the judge asked all of us to stand up and hold up our right hands. We were sworn in and declared citizens of the United States of America. I was officially an American.

Helen and Jesse announced with pride, "You are now 'Nancy,' and no longer 'Eriko.' You have an American name because you are American. You are not to speak of Matsue, Japan, or being adopted ever again, do you understand?" And they meant it. Being adopted, and becoming a naturalized citizen of the United States of America, became a family secret.

Even though I was completely separated from my native country of Japan and my heritage, I cherish my American citizenship, and I am thankful for all the privileges and the freedom I am blessed to have. Our soldiers, past and present, have fought and continue to fight for our precious gift of freedom. Many of them have paid for this gift with their lives.

Another citizenship even more important to me is my citizenship in God's kingdom. I didn't have to study. There were no exams. I didn't have to pay a price. Christ paid it for me.

Another Lesson

Remember my first drink with Matsue? Well, not only did I learn to eat with a fork, sit on a commode, and sleep in a bed, I also learned how to drink. Although Jesse was not a big drinker, he would occasionally drink his Jack Daniels whiskey when his friends would come to play poker, bridge, or pinochle with him.

"I'll beat you in poker tonight, Jess. Might as well bring out our friend Jack now." His army buddies filled the house with crude jokes and the smell of cigars, sweat, and whiskey. Occasionally, I was given my own whiskey so I would remain quiet and out of sight. Helen, meanwhile, would sit with the wives and sip Mogen David wine. After all, ladies don't drink whiskey, and wine is proper, right? To keep me out of the way, Helen would give me a very generous glass of wine. It was a great way to keep me invisible and away from the adults.

3

Pills

HELEN ALSO INTRODUCED me to another form of escape: the emotional escape through prescription drugs. Helen believed she had many ailments. She would often say, "I have to go to the doctor. I think I may have cancer." Here's another one: "The doctor thinks I may have a brain tumor."

Years later, I learned Helen was probably a hypochondriac. She had many emotional scars from seeing firsthand the pain and suffering of World War II and the aftermath of the ravages of war.

For as long as I knew her, Helen had a shoebox filled with prescription medication. She was absolutely obsessed with her bodily functions. Helen would mark her calendar each time there was anything physical to note: aches, pain, bowel movements, etc. She wrote it all down. "I don't remember what time I had my last BM," she would say. Or, "I have to write down when my last (you fill in the blank) happened."

Not only did Helen abuse her medication, but she also took what was occasionally prescribed for me. She had pills to sleep, pills to wake up, pills to calm her nerves, pills to hype her up, and pills for her aches and pains. Her entire day revolved around her pill schedule.

It's so tragic. Helen needed help desperately, but she sought the wrong kind of help. She didn't have a relationship with Christ. She was so lonely and found comfort and purpose in drugs. Later in life, I did, too.

To further her belief in the miracles of drugs, Helen frequently took me to the medical hospital at the army base whether I needed medical attention or not. Helen took me to the doctors with regularity for illnesses that didn't exist, for coughs, colds, aches, and pains she believed I had. "Nancy, you look pale. I think you're coming down with something," she would say.

Helen would describe symptoms to the doctors she wanted me to have in order to get the medication she needed for herself. The doctors wrote prescriptions for nonexistent ailments. Doctors can only go by what we tell them. Helen gave the appearance of being such a dedicated, caring mother to her newly adopted child. Who would question a mother's concern?

The one physical ailment I did have was deafness in my left ear and 70 percent hearing loss in my right ear. However, this was not diagnosed until several years later. I would get frequent ear infections. A high fever was left untreated when I lived in Japan and probably damaged my ears. To date, I have had fourteen ear operations, but none have been able to completely restore my hearing.

The doctors often prescribed pain pills for me after my frequent operations, and during my weeks of recovery in the hospital. Morphine drips were used as well. No wonder I leaned toward pain medication and alcohol for relief. The physical feelings were so familiar and comforting. The relaxed, easy, carefree existence of not feeling emotions or caring was the reward. It worked for a while, until it didn't.

I frequently used pills to withdraw. After all, they seemed to work fine for Helen. Pain pills helped me to coast, and they allowed to me take the yelling, screaming, and criticism in stride. The pills made me indifferent. When I didn't have pills, I had a glass or two (or three or four) of Helen's wine.

Will You Be My Friend?

The first school I attended in the United States (or anywhere for that matter) was in Lompoc, California. I felt lonely, abandoned, and isolated in this strange city and country. I had trouble comprehending a lot of things because of my deafness and inability to understand the English language. I wanted desperately to have a friend.

Even though Helen was trilingual, I wanted someone other than she to teach me the American language. Because her father was French and served as a consulate to the Japanese Embassy, Helen spoke Japanese, French, and English. However, Helen lacked patience and used harsh words. Her criticism scorched my soul.

One day, I was sitting by myself in front of our house, playing a game of jacks. A group of girls about my age approached. I had already learned an important phrase from Helen, and I used this phrase with this group of girls. In wide-eyed wonder, and with a big smile of anticipation on my face, I stood up and asked, "Will you be my friend?" They looked at each other, pointed at me, and walked away laughing. This was *not* the response I was hoping for. I felt the intense pain of rejection, isolation, and abandonment. I felt so different and alone.

That evening, I looked out my window at Mr. Moon, who not long ago helped me find my way, and wondered how long it would take me to get home if I started to walk and follow the moon. I cried myself to sleep in silence.

School Daze

Mrs. Hutchinson was tall and thin. Half-rimmed glasses sat on her sharp, pointed nose. She wore her gray hair in a tight bun. Mrs. Hutchinson was my first-grade teacher and she was mean.

One day, Mrs. Hutchinson asked me, "If you have a dollar and lunch costs thirty-five cents, how much change will you get?"

After what seemed like hours, with everyone staring at me—the new kid in class—I answered with uncertainty. "Fifty cents?" Well, of course, that was the wrong answer.

Once again, I was ridiculed and made fun of, not only by the other students, but also by the teacher. They didn't understand translating English to Japanese and vice versa was a process for me. In addition, no one at that time, including me, knew I was hearing impaired. Mrs. Hutchinson knew I was half Japanese and called me a "stupid Jap." I wanted desperately to curl up within myself and disappear.

I did not share this humiliation with either Helen or Jesse for fear of more ridicule. I kept silent. From then on, the only place I spoke to anyone was at home, and that was only when I absolutely had to.

The voices in my head started to keep me company. Unbeknownst to me, the spiritual warfare had begun. I would lay awake in bed, looking up at the moon for comfort. Then, I would sneak into the kitchen for a little Mogen David wine to warm my body and quiet the voices so sleep would find me.

The next year, Jesse was mercifully transferred to Washington state, where I began second grade. The move was an improvement of sorts. I still would not talk or speak in class for fear of the ridicule that would certainly follow. Thankfully, my new teacher, Mrs. Walker, was very kind and patient.

"Look at these coins," Mrs. Walker would say. "Count them out for me." She showed me pictures of American coins and worked with me to teach me the value of each coin. She spent a lot of time with me, one on one, and helped me in so many ways. I remember her kindness. She left a beautiful impression on my heart of how a teacher is *supposed* to be.

However, because of my "inability" to speak or seemingly understand, I did poorly in school, even with the help of Mrs. Walker. "She needs to be in a special class so she can learn at her ability level," Mrs. Walker said to my parents. "It's not fair to her. She can't keep up, even though I know how hard she is trying. Her tests show an IQ level that indicates mental retardation."

They decided to put me in a special school located in a building apart from the main campus. This building was painted bright red as if to send a bold signal that screamed, "Stupid children go here!" Everyone called this building the "Little Red Schoolhouse." Everyone in the community knew the "retards" went to the Little Red Schoolhouse.

No one put two and two together. I was still learning the English language, so no one suspected I was hearing impaired. Only the voices in my head understood. They were my companions and spoke to me all the time. They did not ridicule me. "You are smarter than they are," the voices would say. "They'll get what's coming to them!" The voices shouted during the day, and they talked to me in my sleep so my nights were restless and fitful.

The isolation, the rejection, the loneliness, and the pain of feeling "different" and not fitting in continued to haunt me. I cared less and less about looking to the moon for direction and light. I only wanted to be companions with the voices in my head and to have the occasional warm drink I snuck during the darkness of night.

Vacation Bible School

Helen and Jesse had a handful of military family friends who persuaded them to let me spend time with others away from my school. They encouraged Helen and Jesse everything would turn out okay if I could only make a few friends. Helen agreed and said, "The children that don't go to Nancy's school won't know how stupid she is."

One family, the Bryants, had five children including Diane, a daughter who was my age. They didn't live in our neighborhood; they had a farm with cows and pigs. The Bryants extended an invitation for me to spend a week with them, and Helen and Jesse said okay. After all, Jesse and Mr. Bryant were in the same military unit. This was a family who could be trusted. Or so we thought.

During my week with the Bryants, Diane's father tried to molest me while I was on my way to use the restroom in the middle of the night. I knew something was wrong and started yelling. He stopped. When everyone woke up from my yelling, Mr. Bryant said, "Nancy is sleepwalking and had a bad dream. She'll be okay." I never told anyone the truth. After all, this must have been *my* fault. I didn't want my friend, Diane, to dislike me. I wanted to be accepted. I didn't want my one and only friend to abandon me. I felt desperation, guilt, and shame. The voices cried out to me, "You will get even with him someday. Just wait!"

A blessing occurred during this same week of my visit with the Bryant family. Diane invited me to attend Vacation Bible School (VBS). At VBS, I was exposed to a different God—a God who loves me! The teachers all smiled and accepted all the children who attended class each day, including me. The teachers talked about a God of forgiveness. They also talked at length about someone named Jesus and about accepting Christ. I didn't understand any of this, but I couldn't wait to go to VBS each day. We sang songs, completed activities, and had fun. I learned to sing songs like "This Little Light of Mine" and "Jesus Loves Me." This was completely different from what I was learning about God through Helen, and I liked it. I was sad when the VBS ended. I knew Helen would not let me attend any church other than a Roman Catholic church. I felt like I had lost a friend when VBS ended. Sadly, it would be many years before I would truly want to learn more about Jesus.

> "More about Jesus would I know,
> More of His grace to others show;
> More of His saving fullness see,
> More of His love Who died for me."
> Verse from "More About Jesus" in Glad
> HALLELUJAHS BY ELIZA E. HEWITT, 1887.

Deaf

Sometime during my second grade school year, we moved to Europe. Prior to our move, I had to have a physical. The doctor said to Helen, "Did you know your daughter is totally deaf in her left ear? In addition, she has very little hearing in her right ear. Nancy is only hearing thirty percent, and that hearing is from her right ear only."

At last, Helen and Jesse came to grips with my physical disabilities and realized I really wasn't stupid. Now, I was just "damaged goods."

"We really made a terrible mistake by adopting Nancy. She is nothing but a problem for us, and she is an embarrassment. I wish we could give her back." I would hear Helen crying and telling Jesse this night after night after night. It's terrible to feel unwanted. Feeling like *you* are the problem damages your life.

One of the towns we lived in during the first year of Jesse's tour in Europe was Idar-Obertstein, a German community. I had to attend a local school where German was the only language spoken except during the English hour when English was taught. My brain was on overload with German to English to Japanese to English to German. My head was a scrambled mess. Plus, I had so much trouble hearing people.

God grants us so many gifts—all undeserved—and I believe the ability to learn multiple languages is truly one of those God-given gifts. Being hearing impaired added to that blessing, because, subconsciously, I was watching people's jaws, lips, eyebrows, and body to put everything together. I was already learning to lip-read. I had no idea God was gently guiding and prodding me to be better prepared for what was to come later in my life.

I quickly learned German and loved the preciseness of the language. Unlike the English language, there were no exceptions to rules ("'I' before 'e' except after 'c' and when it sounds like 'a' as in 'neighbor' or 'weigh,'" etc.).

Because of Jesse's military career, we moved several times while in Europe. As a result, I attended many different schools, bouncing from here to there without much stability, and certainly no great chances of making and retaining friends. I still couldn't fit in, and feelings of isolation engulfed me. The only stability I had were the voices in my head that continued to soothe me, together with the wine, and the whiskey, and the pills. I didn't know at the time all I needed was a love relationship with Jesus.

Eighty-Eight Keys

Helen and Jesse really did try in their own way to help me. To this day, I don't know if I felt loved by them. That is not to say they did not love me. I just didn't feel it. I know they did the best they could.

In an attempt to find *something* I might be good at, Helen said, "How about piano lessons? We found a great piano teacher for you. It will help you learn something new, and you might be good at it." So, she took me to Herr Kopf (which translates to Mr. Head in English), who spoke only German but had the reputation as the best piano teacher in the town. He became my instructor.

Playing the piano paved the way to a safer form of refuge. I was still one crazy, frustrated, mixed-up kid. Although I had been fitted for hearing aids, which helped a little, I was still hearing-impaired and suffering from language whiplash. But with the piano, I was at least a crazy, mixed-up kid with a purpose. I became determined to do whatever it took to be an excellent piano player. I'll make Helen and Jesse proud of me!

After two years of piano lessons, Herr Kopf announced I was playing at the same level as someone who had taken classical piano lessons for at least ten years. He was not known to dole out compliments, so naturally I was thrilled with these words he spoke to Helen and Jesse. (I feel so awkward not calling them my parents, but I just can't seem to call them my parents, and I appreciate you bearing with me.)

Herr Kopf was truly a marvelous instructor with passion and precision. However, his method of correction left a lot to be desired. He used a baton liberally, whacking it across my knuckles every time I made an error. The knuckle whacks were extremely painful. My hands would stay red for the remainder of the day and sometimes until the next morning. To avoid the pain of those knuckle whacks, I often practiced at home for hours and hours. It's no wonder I learned quickly!

I am thankful today for the exposure to music, even though it was sometimes painful. Music was my solace, my comforter, my retreat, and my escape. The piano recitals presented a way for me to express to others the emotions of famous composers that I felt in my soul. I expressed the sorrows, joys, and pain of Chopin, Mozart, and Beethoven through my body and my fingertips. Sadly, neither Helen nor Jesse ever attended any of the recitals. The voices in my head continued their efforts to keep me company, but with music, I at least glimpsed the moon providing a sliver of light in my darkened soul.

I could have been spared a lot of heartache and pain had I learned that inappropriate actions and mistakes bring consequences. With all the "knuckle whacks" life brought, I don't know why I didn't recognize the value of consequences for my actions. Why did I have to keep making the same mistakes over and over again expecting different results? I had developed a Teflon brain, and life lessons just slid right off it.

"I do not understand what I do.
For what I want to do I do not do but what I hate I do."
ROMANS 7:15

Family Secrets

Apart from the exposure to music, living in Europe was not a pleasant experience for me. Helen's infidelity to Jesse—which I was made to witness and participate on several occasions—was too painful. Matsue did what she had to do to provide for me. She kept intimate relationships with several men, but Helen was married, and she did not have to be unfaithful. I was not yet a Christian, but this truly bothered me. She, too, would allow her partner in betrayal to be friendly toward me. I felt so much shame, yet I didn't want to be an embarrassment to Helen, so I would comply with the requests from her lover while Helen silently watched without objection.

In addition, Helen's incessant criticism of me, which started almost immediately following the adoption, escalated as her own guilt engulfed her. She continued to abuse prescription drugs, and Jesse continued to be absent.

The voices stayed with me. They would cry out during the most unsuspecting times of the day. "If you die, you won't feel this pain!" The moon was no longer visible. Where did it go? I could not find my way out of the darkness in my mind.

In Germany, I was also presented with many more opportunities to drink. German contract workers would come to do general repairs in our home as was customary for all the families who lived on base. The workers did not take coffee breaks. Rather, they would take out a beer from their lunch pails and drink it. "*Javol!* It's break time!" The beverage of choice for most Germans was beer, and I acclimated to this cultural habit very quickly, with the ease and grace of a seasoned drinker. For some people, this would not have presented a problem, but it presented a problem for me. I developed an emotional and physical need for beer. Before I turned twelve years old, I was addicted.

While we were in Europe, Helen's daughter, Theresa—Jesse was not her dad—stayed in our Washington house. Theresa had already graduated from high school and was getting married soon. Theresa is another one of the "family secrets." Such "family secrets" can tear the fabric of families apart and rip up pieces of one's soul.

4

Music

In 1962, Jesse's military orders sent us back to Washington. Helen would whine, "I am sick and tired of moving. I don't feel well. What are we going to do with Nancy?" Jesse would go bowling when he couldn't take any more of her constant criticism and complaining. He was often absent. In spite of Helen's frustrations, we headed to American soil once again. After all, orders are orders. If nothing else, Jesse was a good soldier.

By this time, I was in junior high—a difficult time for many students. For me, it was a nightmare. I came back to America with many of the European customs ingrained in me. It was easier for me to communicate in German. When I would meet someone in the school hallway, I would curtsey and shake his or her hand. *"Guten tag,"* ("Good day" in German), I would say. I had a German accent, even when I spoke English.

This brought more ridicule and cruel laughter. "That new girl? She is so weird! She curtsies for God's sake!"

"Can you believe that Nazi?" (Now I'm a Nazi?) "She thinks she's *sooo* cute with that curtsey thing going on."

I felt different and all alone. The voices were getting much louder, and the moon was still absent. Feelings of isolation engulfed me. I couldn't find my way through the darkness.

Helen did try to get help for me. One of her military friends said, "Why don't you let Nancy get involved in music again? Didn't you say she played the piano or something?" Another woman said, "I heard

Nancy sing at church during mass. She has a pretty voice." So, Helen and Jesse found a voice teacher in the neighborhood—I don't recall her name—and I started vocal lessons.

Even though I was very hard of hearing, music continued to be my solace. I could hear the notes in my head. Singing was a wonderful outlet—I could use my voice! I wasn't permitted to use my voice at home to speak my mind or express my opinion. Singing was a great way to express myself with sad songs, angry songs, and yes, even happy melodies sometimes. My voice even helped drown out the voices in my head.

Dog Days

Neither Helen nor Jesse really cared to listen when I practiced at home, but we had a little black poodle, Fifi, who would lie under the piano bench while I sang and played. At that time, Fifi was my only friend and the only one who seemed to even notice I had a voice. It's truly amazing I was unopposed to Fifi being near me. It had taken a long time for me to recover from my fear of dogs. This fear of our four-legged friends began while we still lived in Lompoc, California.

When I was in the first grade, Jesse and Helen had a German Shepherd named Rusty. Rusty was quite beautiful with orange and brown fur mixed with white. I was very frightened of him because I had never seen a dog before, and Rusty was very big. Jesse would laugh maliciously and instruct Rusty to "sic her." When he would jump on me, Rusty could put his front paws on my shoulders easily. Jesse knew how very frightened I was of Rusty. He would say, "It's just a dog! Don't be such a scaredy cat!"

More than likely, Jesse probably would not have allowed Rusty to bite or hurt me, and was just trying to get me to like Rusty. But then again, Jesse did have a warped sense of humor. Thankfully, when we moved to Germany, Rusty stayed behind with Theresa and was eventually given away to a good home. My fear of dogs stayed with me until we returned to Washington, and Helen adopted Fifi.

My lack of friends and my lack of self-esteem caused me bouts of tremendous depression. My consumption of alcohol, a depressant, worsened my despair. The constant struggle with isolation and the voices in my head were becoming more and more problematic. I couldn't seem to keep the voices quiet for very long even when I wanted to. "You like thinking evil thoughts. You want to hurt Helen and Jesse. Go ahead... Do it!" The voices told me I should die. "You're better off dead. Helen, Jesse, the whole world would be better off without you!" At times, the voices seemed to scream at me, full of anger and hate, filling me with those same emotions. Spiritual warfare was taking place, and I wasn't even a Christian When this constant battle exhausted me, I tried to permanently escape the voices by way of suicide. One attempt included Fifi.

I was causing so many problems, and Helen and Jesse would get along just fine if it weren't for me. Helen would frequently remind me of this—she agreed with the voices in my head, and she didn't even know about them! I truly believed her. (It's all about me, right?) The voices in my head that were once my friends turned on me, and they were now reinforcing dangerous messages.

Helen had never learned to drive, so she depended on Jesse for transportation. "Take me to the store. I have to buy groceries. You never do anything for us. The least you can do is take me to the store." Jesse didn't speak much. He knew whatever he said, she would counter with an argument of some sort. So, he took her to the store.

Fifi and I were alone, except for the voices. I felt depleted and defeated. I had no joy and no friends. I didn't care if the moon was visible or not. I no longer felt the need or the desire to find my way home.

I helped myself to Helen's trusty shoebox of prescription drugs, washing the pills down with Mogen David wine. The voices faded away, and I drifted off to sleep. The feelings of loneliness and despair subsided. My brain quieted down. A blanket of white sheltered my mind. The voices were only whispering now.

Fifi was a well-trained, obedient dog, but she must have sensed something was wrong. She knew the rules of the house and usually never got on the sofa or recliner, nor on the chairs or on the beds. Fifi was not allowed to go into any of the bedrooms, including mine. However, she pushed opened my bedroom door, which did not have a lock and could not be closed all the way. My four-legged friend got on my bed and bounced and jumped up and down as I was drifting off. "Please stop. You're making me sick, Fifi." I whimpered. Her rambunctious activities woke me up and caused me to become nauseous. When I vomited, up came all those pills I had swallowed.

"Oh, God! Why did you let me live? Why are you doing this? Can't you see I just want to die? Can't you see I just want to sleep? If there is a god, let me die!" I realize now God had a plan for me, just as He has a plan for you. Of all things, He used a dog to save my life. Indeed, God can use anything He wants to fulfill His purpose. Knowing this, I've come to love dogs.

Many years later, my husband, Randall, had a Dachshund aptly named Dach. Dach was also a lifesaver. On at least two occasions, while I was pulling weeds in our yard, Dach sensed the presence of a snake, gently put his mouth on my wrist to pull it away, and then went after the snake.

A few weeks after Dach died at the age of fourteen, we adopted our Jack Russell terrier. Guess what we named him? Jack, of course. Aren't we clever with the name thing? Jack also protected me from snakes and saved my life several times. Jack and Dach both had several trips to the vet to get anti-venom drugs. Unfortunately, Jack died of cancer after we had him for only seven years.

We missed both dogs very much and had been without one for several years when my husband surprised me with a yellow Lab named Little Miss Haley, who is amazing! We had to change her name to Bailey, but that's another story. Bailey weighs about ninety-four pounds. When my husband is not at home, she stays with me and walks with me wherever I go around the house. Bailey has become my "hearing aid." Without any training, she has taken on the role of a service dog. She alerts me to sounds, doorbells, buzzers, etc. She protects me. Bailey is my companion and my friend. The vet bills due to her allergies and her special dietary requirements are worth every dollar spent.

All pet owners can appreciate the quirks and unique personalities of their pets. Bailey, although no longer a puppy, loves to eat paper. She will go as far as digging in trash cans to find just the right piece of paper to eat. Lately, she has been eating the core from paper towel rolls and rolls of toilet tissue. One day, I came home to find the bathroom door open and toilet paper—what was left of a brand new roll—strewn about the floor. The core was gone. At least she has outgrown eating socks. I just have to be sure to close all doors before leaving for work. Bailey is almost ten. We know her days are numbered, so we cherish our time with her and spoil her rotten.

A Real Cut-Up

Helen always made sure I was dressed well, and I know she wanted to be proud of me. She made sure everything looked perfect on the outside. Helen purchased matching skirts, blouses, sweaters, and shoes for me. Back then, Bobbie Brooks, a very popular brand, was her favorite. I didn't have much say in what kind of clothes I wore. Helen would say, "You can't pick out your own clothes. It's our money, so we decide. Besides, you don't know what looks good and what doesn't." Once again, I had no voice, except the voices in my head.

It was important no one should see the truth about our family. All outward appearances had to be top-notch. Thus, the piano and singing lessons had to come from only the best teachers, and I had to have only the best clothes to wear. After all, it was a reflection on her as a mother, wasn't it? "This is our daughter. Doesn't she look good?" At any rate, I had a closet full of Bobbie Brooks skirts and sweaters.

I was often sent to my room if I expressed an opinion. I wasn't allowed to have my own ideas. Okay, maybe sometimes I talked back, too. I was to be seen, not heard. Often, I was not even seen.

"Go to your room! I'm sick and tired of you arguing with me. When I say 'no,' it means 'no'! I don't owe you an explanation, and I'm sick and tired of looking at you!"

Jesse left for the bowling alley, and I headed toward my room. A pair of scissors on top of the kitchen table beckoned me, so I grabbed them on the way. The matching clothes also beckoned to me. I went into the closet, where I felt safe—a reminder of the safety I felt when I used to hide in our outhouse in Japan. The color-coordinated sweaters, skirts, and blouses were all hanging so neatly. I couldn't take it anymore—all this perfection! So I ripped the clothes off their hangers and let them fall on the closet floor. Snip by snip, I started cutting up my clothes.

The voices in my head, now three of them, took their turns speaking loudly, each screaming to be heard. "Go! Cut faster! Shred them to bits!" I looked on the otherwise immaculate floor and saw the ruin. Was it worth the punishment I received afterward? At the time, I thought it was. The voices quieted down. It seemed the only way to keep them at bay was to destroy and inflict damage.

Besides snatching alcohol here and there, I found a more readily available means of keeping the voices silent and dealing with the pain of ridicule. I would pick at my arm, and then scratch it up severely until it would bleed. To feel purged of the evil I felt lived in me was a warm and welcome relief.

Unfortunately, what started as a mere itch on my arm would often turn into a big gash that would become infected. Helen would rush me to the doctor. "You have an unknown disease," she would say. "We have to get you treated! You could spread the disease to us, and that would be horrible!" The doctor would reassure her I was not contagious. A mosquito or spider bite had caused an itch I had scratched, and subsequently, the wound became infected. "Just put this antibiotic cream on it, keep it clean, and Nancy will be fine." The doctors did not have a clue I wanted to bleed; I needed to bleed.

The pain of self-inflicted injuries was a soothing relief for me. The pain helped me to focus away from the emotional wounds that swallowed me on the inside—the pain of abandonment, isolation, loneliness, and rejection. I preferred this self-inflicted pain over the emotional pain inflicted by Helen and others. When I bled, I felt purged of all the emotional pain. I felt cleansed.

In 2005, one of my very earliest clients who came for counseling at our center was a young preteen who was cutting herself. I'll call her Jane. Jane was a beautiful, intelligent young girl who told me she felt ugly and was in tremendous emotional pain. After our first session, I thought, *Oh God! I've never had a cutter as a client, and I don't know what to do! Help!* And He did. He helped me to remember how I felt when I was a teen, and He gave me empathy for this young lady. After many sessions of counseling, Jane graduated from high school and college. She is a very successful businesswoman today. Jane has come by often to update me on her life. She recently became engaged and plans to marry her high-school sweetheart soon. Her contagious laughter and engaging joy are miracles to behold.

The majority of children who are adopted today are blessed with loving, nurturing parents. These parents lavish them with guidance and shower them with love, and the children grow accordingly. I believe my circumstance was one God allowed me to have, so He could mold me and draw me closer to Him.

God is the great God of "what if's." What if I had had a "normal" upbringing? What if I was never physically or sexually abused or raped? What if I hadn't been hard of hearing and then became deaf? I can't help but wonder whether or not I would have rejected the idea of desperately needing my Lord and Savior. I can't help but wonder if I would be even more self-centered than I am. I know today I am grateful for Helen and Jesse. They did the best they could with what they had. If it were not for the pain in my life, I would not have the exuberant joy that fills me today, and perhaps, I would have never founded our counseling center. God is the only one who knows.

Shirley's Ghost

Helen had another daughter, Shirley, who died at the tender age of nine, before I was adopted. Like my adoptive sister, Theresa, Shirley was not Jesse's daughter—yet another family secret. Jesse was, however, the one who physically carried Shirley to the hospital when her appendix ruptured. She died within minutes of arriving at the hospital. According to Jesse and Theresa, Helen wanted to adopt a child to replace the one she had lost. Helen chose me.

I could never measure up to Shirley. It was very upsetting for me to be surrounded by pictures of her everywhere we lived—California, Europe, and Washington. I could not escape her. I could not escape Shirley's ghost.

Jesse was hardly ever home. He wasn't home to hear the constant criticism about my grades, my looks, or my talents (or lack thereof). The voices in my head would also torment me and remind me repeatedly how I could not measure up to Shirley. To this day, I am still perplexed by how someone competes with a dead person.

"We made such a mistake adopting you, Nancy," Helen would say. "You are nothing like Shirley used to be. You are such a disappointment! In fact, you'll grow up to be just like your mother—a tramp and a whore." She spoke these words so often they became ingrained in my spirit. The multiple voices in my head agreed with Helen. All the while, Jesse continued to go bowling. No one was there to console, reassure, or reaffirm me. I had no friends, not even the voices for they had become my adversaries. I no longer cared whether the moon lit my way or not. The hurting had to be stopped, and soon.

Womanhood

The saying, "Sticks and stones may break my bones, but words can never hurt me," is a lie. Ask any child who is being bullied at school. Ask any adult who is experiencing professional bullying in the workplace. Ask me how cruel and vicious words can be.

At the tender age of nine, I journeyed into womanhood. I did not understand what was happening. We had not yet discussed this topic during our health class at school. Helen and I had not had this talk about the female body. My first menstrual cycle began at home around ten-thirty at night. My curdling scream could have been heard across the street if the windows had been open. Helen came rushing to my room. When she saw the evidence of my womanhood, she immediately began yelling at me. "You are a sinner! God is punishing you for being such a tramp. If you weren't so bad, God wouldn't allow this to happen until you are thirteen! You're going to hell for sure!"

I felt guilt, humiliation, and shame. The voices in my head shrieked on top of each other for prominence, telling me I deserved to be punished. They grew louder and louder, and the moon that guided me years ago was gone forever. My way was lost for good—or so I thought.

"For the Son of Man came to seek and to save the lost."
LUKE 19:10

5

Cheater, Cheater!

IN THE MIDST of all this emotional havoc, I was mercifully granted a glimpse of hope in junior high school: I had learned to make a few friends. They were all male. I didn't know how to have female friends yet. I thought they were all cruel with their words like Helen, and I couldn't trust females. So, I had lots of boyfriends.

Ben was one of my boyfriends. He was very kind to me. Through the miracle of social media, we recently reconnected, and he shared with me a memory he had of Jesse. Ben used to ride his bike over to our house to visit. Often, it would get too dark for him to ride his bike home, so Jesse would put his bike in the trunk and drive him home. Jesse could be kind in his own gruff way. I am grateful Ben reminded me not all of Jesse's actions were mean and hurtful. Some were kind.

While attending Hudtloff Junior High, I joined the choir. Mike and I sang duets, and we became good friends. Mike and his friend Gene would come over to our house and spend time with me. They were like my big brothers. I had a crush on one of them and then the other. They both seemed to look after me, and Jesse didn't chase them off with his gruff ways.

Mike and Gene would come over to play croquet with Jesse and me. Of course, Jesse would cheat. When he thought no one was looking, he would kick his ball closer to the wicket. I guess we all knew he cheated, and we let him win. I am smiling as I write this. Perhaps

Jesse is smiling too. Jesse didn't like to lose, and he did what was needed to win.

On Christmas Eve, Helen would drop me off at the Roman Catholic church for midnight mass, something very important to Helen. She also stressed the importance of going to confession and doing my penance, which I did blindly each week. During the Lenten season, it was deemed necessary for me to confess and do penance on a daily basis. After midnight mass, Jesse and Helen would say, "Okay, you can open one of your two gifts now, and the other in the morning." I would select one of the packages, open it, and then drink a glass of Mogen David wine with Helen. That's what Christmas meant to me growing up: confessions, penance, going to mass alone, opening a present, and drinking wine with Helen afterward. How sad is that?

One Christmas, I received the game of Monopoly. I was so thrilled when Jesse agreed to play the game with me. I should have known better. Guess what? He swore, —— it! These dice are deformed!" Then he stormed off to bed because he was losing. We never played Monopoly again. Jesse did not like to lose.

Jesse took me fishing once. There was some sort of trout tournament at the lake on the army base. The good news and bad news is I caught more fish than Jesse. He never took me fishing again. Jesse did not like to lose.

Because Jesse didn't take me fishing anymore, I went on my own. I don't know where my love of fishing came from. Perhaps it is a remnant of the fond memories I have toward the fishermen who rescued me. I don't know. Anyway, I would dig up worms behind our house, grab a fishing pole from the garage, and walk to the lake nearby. There was a bridge and an underpass where I would sit and read Robert Frost, Henry Wadsworth Longfellow, Edgar Allen Poe, and other poets while I fished. I don't recall ever catching anything then. But maybe that's why it's called "fishing." My husband reminds me of that when he takes me offshore. Sometimes I don't catch anything offshore either, but fishing is still one of my favorite hobbies.

I am grateful to have learned from Jesse's behavior, although sometimes the process was painful. I learned winning is not what's important. It's not necessarily how you play the game either. It's how you react to losing (or not catching fish) that shows character. I thank Jesse for imparting this important life lesson to me.

"Thou Shalt Not Steal"

One day, on my way to one of my singing lessons, the voices in my head (at least four were competing for my attention by now) said, "You know, you're a teenager now. We think you should be wearing makeup like all the other girls in school. You really stand out. You look different. Heck, you don't even wear a bra, and you *really* need one, big girl!" Do you know how hard it is to keep four voices quiet?

With the exception of a little Vaseline on my eyelashes, I was forbidden to wear makeup. So, naturally, I had to be like everybody else. If I couldn't wear a training bra like the other girls, I could at least wear mascara.

The competing voices in my head gave me detailed, step-by-step instructions. They said, "Skip your voice lessons, and keep the money for beer or wine. Go to the drugstore, and just take the makeup. Come on! Don't be a chicken. You can do this. Maybe this is the *one* thing you can do right!"

I started walking away from my teacher's house and toward the drugstore, which was located on a major street. The voices triumphed. They started to quiet down.

About ten minutes later, I was inside our neighborhood drugstore. Mr. Manley owned the store, which was named—drum roll—"Manley's Drugstore." The voices whispered encouragement to me. "Go on. You're doing great! You can do this!" It was like having my own cheerleading section in my head rooting just for me. I had my own fan club!

As "luck" would have it, Mr. Manley himself happened to be standing at the counter, and he witnessed me stealing the tube of mascara. Although Mr. Manley was not very tall in stature—only about five feet and four inches—he had a big heart. Instead of calling the police, he called Jesse, probably thinking Jesse would lecture me and maybe ground me for life.

"Jesse? This is Mr. Manley. I'm afraid there's been a slight misunderstanding. Your daughter has returned the tube of mascara she took from my store. Will you come pick her up?" He was really trying to give me a break, not realizing Jesse would punish me severely—not just ground me for life.

When Jesse arrived, he was livid. With his face scrunched up and his jaws clenched, he called the police and insisted they put me in juvenile detention over the two-day weekend.

"Jesse, let's think this through," said Mr. Manley. "No harm is done. She has returned the mascara. Just ground her from going out for a few weeks. I'm sure she has already learned it's wrong to steal." Mr. Manley begged Jesse, but Jesse would have none of it.

Believe me, being carted off and spending the weekend in juvie was the most humiliating experience ever. The smell and the company were too overwhelming to comprehend. "Hey you, new girl, why are you here? Score some weed? Are you hooking?" Even their questions were appalling. The girls cursed, spat, and ridiculed me. Once again, I didn't seem to fit in.

Did I belong anywhere? I felt isolation, rejection, guilt, and shame. These emotions were the theme of my life. I wondered how Helen felt about what had happened. Was she relieved I was out of the house? What would Matsue think? Is ending up in juvie what my mother would have wanted? Is this my better life in America? I was really lost and couldn't find my way.

Jesse picked me up after the weekend and brought me home. I never heard about the "incident" from them ever again. Neither he nor Helen spoke a word about it. But the voices in my head talked to me and congratulated me. "You did great! We didn't think you had it in you. Way to go!" I kept such good company, didn't I?

As far as I can recall, that is the only time I have stolen anything from anyone. I learned from this experience there are consequences to stealing. I finally learned there are consequences to all my actions.

Sadly, just because I knew this didn't mean my future was free of more stupid, insane actions, and the resulting consequences.

High School

After the ninth grade, I somehow managed to get into yet another school. Music, pills, and booze became my constant companions, along with the voices in my head. By this time, I had lost my German accent and customs, which enabled me to feel more accepted. Through the caring guidance of schoolteachers and the support of faculty, I excelled in vocal music competitions and even received some music awards. Consequently, I earned some positive recognition and made a few friends in the process.

One of my friends, Sue, sang with me in a girls' ensemble. She was one of the few friends who knew I never had a birthday party. Sue took the opportunity to throw a surprise party for me at her house. She invited all of our choir members to a swimming-pool birthday bash, complete with plenty of alcohol. Did I mention her parents were not at home? Needless to say, we swam and we partied. Sadly, I'm the one who doesn't remember very much of this. During my one and only birthday party growing up, I blacked out from drinking. It's a wonder I even remember I was given a birthday party.

My choir director was Mr. Edward Harmic. At that time, I did not value the positive impact he made on my life and the lives of other students. He went the extra mile, visiting parents, driving his students who didn't have transportation to various concerts, and he was (and still is) such an encourager.

Mr. Harmic gave me opportunities to not only sing solos in high school, but also to sing at his Lutheran church on Sunday mornings. On one of those Sundays, I realized once again not everyone worships in the same way. The service brought back happy memories of Vacation Bible School with my friend Diane.

As a Roman Catholic, Helen ensured I had proper Catholic doctrine and punctual, steady church attendance, even though she only attended mass at Christmas and Easter. Catholicism works well for many, but Helen's view of God was very unhealthy. The God I came to know through her was an angry, stern, and vengeful God who punishes. For me, Catholicism was about performance and rituals.

Hearing the sermons at Mr. Harmic's church intrigued me. I would hear about God's love and His forgiveness, compassion, and mercy. Decades would pass before I truly understood these concepts.

"The Lord is gracious and righteous;
our God is full of compassion."
PSALM 116:5

Temper, Temper

Jesse's explosive temper cost me a few tearful nights and embarrassing days during high school. One evening, my parents had a horrible fight. It was more than the usual yelling, cursing, and screaming. "Why don't you quit your d--n yelling?" Helen screamed.

Jesse countered, "Because all you do is nag, nag, nag. You don't listen to anyone but yourself!"

Helen then blamed me for her unhappiness. "If it weren't for Nancy, I would have walked out on you years ago!" Then, the blows followed.

I am not certain as to who threw the first physical punch, although I know Helen launched the verbal assault. I tried to intervene, and in the process, I caught a blow across my nose. With a black eye and a broken nose, I was a sight to behold. To this day, I have a very prominent nose. I don't know if Jesse intended to hurt me that badly, but I know he did not appreciate my interference.

I had to ride the bus to school until I saved enough money through babysitting to buy my first car, a Chevrolet Biscayne. I felt embarrassed and self-conscious about my face on the bus the next morning. When asked how I got the black eye and broken nose, I lied about what actually happened and told people I ran into a door. I became adept at lying.

Through forgiveness and healing, I have found solace. Jesse did not know any other way to discipline. He did what he knew. He told me as a child he, too, was often struck. To him, administering physical harm equaled discipline, which equaled love. That doesn't mean it's the right way.

Did this experience teach me to stay out of other people's battles, especially physical ones, and to mind my own business? No. Sadly, chaos became a way of life for me. I often searched for ways to get involved.

Jesse and Helen taught me life lessons I internalized: Physical harm equals love. I have to be invisible. I *am* invisible. I am not important. My opinions are worthless.

Thus far, life was not all that great with Helen and Jesse. Again, I did not feel safe. Once again, guilt, isolation, rejection, and shame clothed me in darkness.

Buckle Up

Up until the age of thirteen, I would get spankings with the brass buckle of Jesse's army belt. The humiliation was unbearable. "You know what to do. Get in position!" He would instruct me as if I were one of his charges in the army. This meant I had to be naked and bent over, grabbing my ankles. The last time he spanked me "in position," I was in a woman's way. I think he realized he had gone too far for too long. That was the last time he spanked me.

I often had welts no one could see. The blisters would take days to heal and made it difficult for me to sit down. The emotional scars took years to mend.

I am not saying spanking your child is wrong. (Proverbs 13:24) I believe it is ok to use spanking to discipline a child in the way he or she should go. However, anger should not be the force and catalyst for discipline.

Iron Out Your Problems

Jesse was not the only one who inflicted physical discipline. Helen did, too. She also used her tongue to inflict verbal and emotional abuse. Back in those days, I don't think people even had labels for this.

"Make sure you put razor sharp creases in those pant legs," Helen would remind me with her scream. I was expected to iron Jesse's army fatigues, and they had better be starched and pressed to pass military inspection. If the fatigues were not ironed properly, Helen would burn me with the tip of the hot iron in places that were not visible. She also told me how worthless and stupid I was. "You can't do anything right like Shirley could." She would often tell me, "If it weren't for you, Jesse and I would have divorced years ago. I regret the day we adopted you. You're damaged goods!" Later, I would grab a glass of Jack Daniels and have a drink to quiet the voices and help block the pain.

I wanted to be invisible and to disappear. Neither Jack Daniels nor the voices could help me to like me. I immersed myself in feelings of worthlessness nothing could drown out.

It's "iron"ic I love to press my husband's clothes today. I find this very therapeutic. Occasionally, I'll post on social media I'm relaxing and ironing my honey's clothes. The feedback I often get is, "Are you insane?" No, I'm not. Today, I am sane and sober.

I was determined to break the cycle of physical and emotional abuse I endured as a child. I wanted my children to learn a different way. I know I was not a perfect mom when my children were young— far from it. But I pray they have some good memories along with the bad. I pray they have come to know and understand I did the best I was able to do under the circumstances. I pray they are quicker to forgive me of my wrongdoings than I was to forgive Matsue, Helen, and Jesse. For me, freedom to experience joy comes from the freedom to choose forgiveness.

"Bear with each other and forgive one
another if any of you has a grievance
against someone. Forgive as the Lord forgave you."
COLOSSIANS 3:13

Help! We're Locked In!

Some may remember a trio that was very popular in the sixties called Peter, Paul, and Mary. I was blessed to have been part of the Dennis, John, and Nancy trio. After John graduated from school, Vic joined our group in his stead. We were a family, and we were quite good. We had a great sound. We sang in neighboring restaurants and civic groups. It's too bad we did not have the wisdom to record some of our music.

Recently, through social media, I was able to reconnect with Dennis and ask him for some insight about our group. Dennis recalled one particular adventure I want to share.

After one Saturday practice session, Dennis and I went out with John and a female friend of his. I was a junior in high school at that time. We ended up hanging out at a park located within the grounds of Western State Mental Hospital. This was a beautiful place—very calm with lots of whispering trees and color-dotted flowers. Time flew by, and, all of a sudden, it was pitch-dark. We had to get home. All of us would get in trouble if we were out past our curfew. Little did we know the gates to the state hospital grounds were locked after dusk. We drove around for a long period of time, looking for any possible way out. After all, we were locked up within the confines of a state mental hospital. Yikes!

Finally, after several attempts, we found an unlocked gate and were able to leave. This would make a perfect setting for a great horror movie, don't you think? Dennis told me he got in a lot of trouble from his dad for coming home so late. I don't remember what happened to me, but I think it was bad.

I cherish the times together with my trio, and I wouldn't trade anything for these memories. There was a dimension of love and friendship that was a once-in-a-lifetime adventure. Someday, God willing, I hope we can have a reunion and sing together again, even if it means we get together and sing for Him in Eternity. The good news is, if we do have an earthly reunion, I won't know if I'm off-key or not. I can sing just for the joy of singing. Being deaf comes with blessings, too.

"Come, let us sing for joy to the Lord; let us shout
aloud to the Rock of our salvation."
Psalm 95:1

Black Out

I draw a blank when it comes to the details—who, what, when, where, why, and how—of some of my adventures during my senior year in high school. For example, one evening I was watching Ray Charles perform at a club. I remember the sound of peanut shells crushing under the weight of the crowd who came to listen. I was sitting with a group of people totally unknown to me. I was in San Francisco! To this day, I still don't know how in the world I ended up there or who brought me and why.

After the club closed, a group of us went to a house. All of us gathered on the floor around a large, round table. Everyone, including me, took turns passing around a pipe from which we inhaled deeply for a long time. At the time, I didn't know what was in the pipe. I just wanted to belong and to fit in. Well, that pipe contained heroin. Before long, I was transported into another dimension.

Thankfully, I was absolutely terrified of what heroin did to me. I liked it immediately and knew if I took heroin again, I would surely be hooked. It was so powerful I stayed away from it. I know God was at work, preventing me from becoming a heroin addict. Even before I knew Christ as my Lord and Savior, God was watching out for me and keeping me from the "what if's."

Eventually, I was back in Washington, somehow safe and back in school. How did I get back? Good question. My trip to San Francisco was indeed another blackout. My sixteenth birthday party at Sue's house was probably the first. Sadly, this pattern of having blackouts became a part of my life thanks to alcohol and drugs.

The military base had a theater arts group I participated in frequently while in high school. Although I was in several plays and musicals, again neither Helen nor Jesse attended any of my performances. One play in particular, *A Funny Thing Happened on the Way to the Forum*, was very special because I had the leading female role. Against all hope, I prayed either Helen or Jesse—dare I even pray for both— would come to watch the last performance of the season. All of us in the theater group had worked so hard, and the performance would testify to our efforts. Neither Helen nor Jesse was in the audience.

In my dressing room, I noticed a bottle of Jack Daniels whiskey. Where did that bottle come from? I don't recall. I do remember, however, I drank most of it before actually going on stage. How did the play go? Did my understudy take my place? I don't know. It's probably a good thing I can't remember. This was another blackout. Sadly, there would be more to come.

"Be careful, or your hearts will be weighed down with carousing, drunkenness and the anxieties of life, and that day will close on you suddenly like a trap."
Luke 21:34

6

Grace

BY THE GRACE of God, I managed to get through school and actually graduate. Most of my graduating class had family members in attendance. I did not. When the announcer called my name, and I started to walk forward, I tripped over my own two feet and fell. Interestingly enough, my American name "Nancy" means "grace" or "graceful." I did not live up to my name. *Everyone* saw me fall. I picked myself up off the floor and kept walking, one step at a time, until I got to the prize: my coveted diploma. This was my ticket out.

California, Here I Come—Again!

After the ceremony, many of the graduates celebrated in different ways. I celebrated as well, although I don't remember any of the details. In all likelihood, alcohol was involved. Meanwhile, the voices in my head continued to fill me with anger, bitterness, resentment, and self-pity. As hard as I tried, I couldn't drink enough to make the voices go away.

California was a familiar place. So, much to the anger of Helen and Jesse, I enrolled in the University of California, Los Angeles, thanks to a music education scholarship. They wanted to keep me at home (even though they wanted me gone), but I knew I had to get away. "Bewildered," "floundering," and "immature" describe me back then pretty well. Instead of focusing on my classes, I was more focused on where to find a bar, and who to drink with, and what time we would start. Those concerns started to rule my life.

One evening, after being at a bar (and, of course, lying about my age), I was walking back to the campus alone. This was not the only time I had put myself in dangerous situations. I was approached by a male who had been at the bar. He attacked, beat, and sexually assaulted me. A trial ensued. Based on my taped testimony and several eyewitnesses, this man was court-martialed. I don't know any other details.

The shame was too much. Helen and the voices were right—I was a tramp. Now, I really was damaged goods. Going back to school was totally out of the question, so I crawled back to Washington, once again filled with shame and guilt. I went back to Helen and Jesse's house.

It didn't take long to see what a horrible mistake returning home was. The verbal cruelty was worse than before. Helen had plenty to say about the assault. "You probably asked for it. After all, you're a tramp. You're turning out just like your mother." I had had enough. I hadn't completely unpacked my bags, which made leaving again much easier. *This* time I was leaving for good.

That same week, I headed for the train station in Tacoma, Washington, not far from where we were living. A friend came to pick me up at the house as I had sold my car for travel money. On to bigger and better things! I was headed to El Paso, Texas. Why El Paso? Good question.

Because I was so full of myself and so smart, there was only one logical thing a smart person like me would do. A flat map of the United States was on the table in front of me. I closed my eyes and put my finger on the map. It landed on El Paso. Isn't this a great way to find your destination? Did I know anyone there? No. Did I have a job lined up? No. Did I have a plan of action? Of course not! Who needs a plan? I had money to burn—about three hundred dollars after I paid for my ticket.

I was ready to take on the world and prove to everyone (Helen and Jesse) I really could make it on my own. I was going to follow the moon! Of course, I had to find it again first. Details, right? Maybe the voices would help me. So would my other faithful friend and companion: Jack Daniels.

The train ride was uneventful, or maybe I don't remember anything except for the fact that most of the money I had was spent on Bloody

Marys (vodka and tomato juice). I had twenty-five dollars tucked away in my billfold—all that remained from the original three hundred. Did I have a drinking problem or what?

My first experience in El Paso is unforgettable. I disembarked the train with my one suitcase, sat on it in the middle of the station, looked around at the crowd of people coming and going—most of them speaking Spanish—and all I could do was cry. I must have been somewhat sober by this time, because I knew things were really messed up. I had no money, no friends, no job, and no hope. All I had was my suitcase, twenty-five dollars, and the voices in my head.

Across from the train station, I saw a large overhead sign that lit up the evening sky. The sign read "Jesus Saves" and provided light for the otherwise darkened street. It hung on the outside of a building that served as a shelter for the homeless. This shelter was similar to the ones you see in many of our major cities today. I think it may have been a Salvation Army shelter, but I'm not sure.

I had twenty-five dollars to my name, all my belongings in one suitcase, and no place to go. I walked over to the shelter and asked for a room. The man behind the desk wore a name-tag that read, "Volunteer Joe."

"Do you have any money at all?" Joe asked me. "If so, a room will cost twenty-five dollars a week or seven dollars a day. A hot meal is included. If you can't pay, that's okay, too."

"Yes, I have money. I can pay for the week," I responded.

Joe said, "If that's all the money you have, you can have the room at no cost. Hang on to it. It may come in handy."

The room was small and sparsely furnished but clean. The common bathroom accommodations were down the hall and shared with the other women on the floor. "We have free, hot meals after worship," said one of the women who had a room down the hall. Well, worship did not interest me, because I didn't know what that meant. But I was hungry and didn't want to appear ungrateful for the accommodations, so I thought, *Why not?*

Other homeless people filled the downstairs room to capacity. I took a seat and listened to the songs and the sermons. I don't remember much about the worship other than the singing was terrible. *I would have shown them how to sing, except none of the songs were familiar.* These songs were not the songs I had learned in the Roman Catholic church. So, I just sat and listened with criticism filling my mind. Here I was: homeless, without work, and at rock bottom. It didn't occur to me for a moment I was at the bottom and looking up, critical of everyone and everything around me. That's pretty sad, isn't it?

> *"Pride goes before destruction, a haughty*
> *spirit before a fall."*
> PROVERBS 16:18

How many times have I looked down on others, thinking I was better than they were? How many times have I judged others by how they were dressed, by what cars they drove, and by whether or not they looked successful? Sadly, I was in the basement, blinded. I was unable to see the stairs right next to me. The stairs were there for me to climb out, but because I was self-absorbed in my pathetic world, I was too blind to see.

"I am going to make it on my own. I don't belong in this place. I have to get out quickly!" The voices agreed with me. One reason I needed to get out of the shelter was the fact that absolutely *no alcohol* was allowed. If anyone was caught with a liquor bottle, that person was *out.* I didn't quite have the guts to sneak a bottle in. Plus, I didn't have any extra money. My pride did not let me get a room for free. I could pay my own way.

Get a Job!
The very next day I did what every red-blooded American would have done. I looked for work. With determination to show the world—Helen and Jesse—I didn't need anyone, I started my job search.

Eureka! I was lucky. The very first place I stepped into hired me. Being drawn to what was familiar, I had walked into a cocktail lounge. Stew, the manager, asked, "Have you ever been a waitress before?" I answered honestly: No, I hadn't. "No problem! Can you dance?"

I lied—lying was becoming second nature to me—and said, "Yes." After all, "Nancy" means "grace," so I went with the flow.

"Turn around and walk for me, slowly," Stew asked. So I did. Stew hired me then and there. Unfortunately, I was pretty naïve.

"Okay, Bambi, show me what you can do."

What? "My name isn't Bambi! My name is Nancy!" I responded. I didn't realize this cocktail lounge was really a strip club. I didn't even know what a strip club was. As wild as I had been during high school, I'd never been inside a place like this.

Now, after lying about my age, I had to dance on the stage. "Dance slow, Bambi. Take your time. Let the music move you. Give them a show! You'll make the tips. Just move while you take your clothes off. Candi (probably not her real name) can show you the ropes. Just watch her, okay?"

I needed a job. I needed to get out of that shelter. I needed a drink. The voices clamored for attention.

Somehow, God's grace was with me, even then, and I just couldn't do it. I just couldn't take my clothes off in front of the small group of men who were already bleary-eyed as they stared at the girls dancing on stage, teasing and enticing them.

"What's the matter with you?" Stew yelled as he banged his fist on the table. Stew was about six feet tall and weighed maybe 190 pounds. All muscle. Was I afraid of him? No, I was more afraid of becoming a person I would hate even more than I already did. I walked out of the club—still jobless, still homeless, and definitely still hopeless. But I had kept my clothes on and held on to what little dignity could be mustered. God once again saved me from the "what if's." He saved me from myself. I just didn't know it yet.

The next day, I started job-searching again. This time, I stayed away from bars as a potential place of employment. I saw a convenience store with a "Help Wanted" sign. I lied about my age again (lying gets easier and easier) and got the job as a cashier. As bad as my math skills were, I did know how to count out change. Chuck, a balding roly-poly of a man, said I had potential and a pleasant personality.

Somehow, chaos seemed to follow me. Because I was cunning, I managed to hide beer behind the counter, and took swigs of it while no one was looking. Chuck trusted me, and I betrayed him by drinking on the job. I was a little hazy, and didn't see the man walking into the store with a cap over his head and a gun in his hand.

"Don't do anything stupid, you ——, or I'll blow your ——ing head off!"

I didn't react quickly enough to push the "panic" police button under the register. "No problem! Here's the money. Take it. It's all yours!" The money wasn't all he was after. After the robbery, the robber took me outside at gunpoint and beat me. The police arrived too late because the unspeakable had already occurred.

I pressed charges against the perpetrator, and the police filed a report. The humiliation and shame continued to follow me. Once again, I had to testify. He was put in prison for about five years. Thankfully, I did not get pregnant from the assault. God was protecting me even when I didn't have a relationship with Him. He had a plan for me. I would see the moon again in its entire splendor. I just had to have a drink and clear my head first. I just had to quiet the voices in my head.

"You're doing a good job for us. I know you had a rough start at the store, but I really appreciate you coming back to work." Chuck was very kind, and he continued to trust me to close the shop. He made a change in policy, requiring two employees at closing time. That put a damper on my ability to sneak drinks here and there.

After a few paychecks, it was time to be on my own *for real*, finally. A lady volunteer who looked like she had been run over by a truck was handling the front desk. What few teeth she had were yellow, but she was smiling and friendly. She said, "Nancy, I sure wish you luck and God's blessing on your life. I will be in prayer for you. I hope I don't see you back here unless it's to volunteer."

Right, count on it! Like I would really want to volunteer here? Huh. I said, "Thank you for letting me stay here," but I thought to myself, *Good riddance!* Thank God I didn't have to listen to that horrible singing anymore.

With my suitcase in hand and seventy-five dollars in my pocket, I went apartment-hunting. I found myself on a street that bordered Juarez, Mexico. Perfect! I had heard tequila was only a quarter a shot glass across the border. Oh, and you could get a shampoo and haircut for seventy-five cents, too. All one had to do was walk across the border, and all the necessities of life could easily be found at inexpensive costs. On this street I found my new refuge. One set of apartments looked superb. It had only about twenty units, laundry accommodations, and a pool.

The leasing agent was an overweight, short woman with matted brown hair, baggy legs, and saggy eyelids. She looked pretty pathetic with a cigarette dangling out of the corner of her mouth, and the smoke curling up toward the ceiling. The rent was only seventy-five dollars a month, which was exactly the amount I had in my pocket. *It's fate!* I thought. I signed a lease for three months and paid for the first month in advance. Look out, world—here I come!

My new apartment had a bed, a small dresser, an end table, a lamp, a coffee table, and a green Formica kitchen table complete with two chairs—all in the same room. One might call this an open-concept floor plan. A small, closet-sized bathroom was separated from the main room by colored hanging beads that swooshed when you walked through the archway. Duct tape held the upholstery together, and the swimming pool was green...from "something" growing in it. Yuck! It wasn't paradise, but it was my very own apartment. It was *my* paradise.

With my own apartment, a job, and the assault behind me, my future was looking pretty good. My job as a cashier was going well, and Chuck, my boss, was good to me. A decent paycheck and my own pad—can't get any better than this! Helen and Jesse would see I can do this on my own. Won't they be proud?! The voices were proud of me and spoke to me often, sometimes suggesting I should drink more. Sometimes, when I did drink "enough," the voices would quiet down.

Wanna Dance?

David, a customer who had come into the convenience store before, stopped by once again. He had a fair complexion and a neat appearance. Outwardly, he looked like the "all-American guy next door," not too tall and not too short. Just right. He walked by the cooler and picked up a six-pack of beer. *Okay, he's got the right idea,* I thought to myself. As he walked over to the counter to check-out and pay, he gave me a large smile and asked me what I thought was a crazy question.

"Do you wanna dance?" He had a deep, east-Texas drawl when he spoke. Huh? Who is this? He must be nuts!

Although David's smile was nice, his teeth looked as if they were potted with minerals. That didn't seem to bother him at all. He kept smiling. "May I see some ID, please?" I asked. I couldn't tell if he was old enough to drink or not. Of course, I was not old enough to be selling beer. Naturally, I had lied about my age to get this job. *One of these days I need to come clean with Chuck, so he doesn't get in trouble,* I thought to myself. After all, Chuck was giving me a chance to make it on my own.

As it turned out, the man with the smile was indeed old enough to drink alcohol. In fact, according to David's driver's license, he had eleven years on me. David continued to come to the store, and our conversations grew in length. Each time, he bought beer—an absolute requirement for someone to date me. It wasn't long before he asked me out.

In September of the same year, David and I married. I was able to quit my job and move out of the apartment with the green pool. I got pregnant within a few months and, for the most part, had a normal pregnancy. I didn't drink during my pregnancy, not because I was such a good mom, but because drinking anything made me very ill. So I stayed off the booze. Once again, God was taking care of me.

I knew something was wrong when my water broke in July. It was hot and dry as only El Paso can be. Someone called an ambulance to take me to the hospital. Where was David? I don't recall. Maybe he was there or maybe he wasn't. This painful time of my life is fuzzy, and it wasn't because of alcohol. Maybe it was from the intense emotional pain.

I really wanted to have this child. I could be a much better mother than Matsue or Helen. It was important for me to have this child, someone who I could truly belong to and be a part of. I was desperately trying to turn my life around. I was even going to church.

Baby Jesse was stillborn. I never got to see him. I never got to hold him. I never got to even grieve his death. After returning to our apartment, I discovered David's mother and family had taken everything from the baby's room. Not a trace of baby things could be found.

I was so very angry! Why did God allow this? Why did He let my baby die? He never even had a chance! Why wasn't I allowed to even grieve?

Everyone acted as if it didn't happen. Was I going crazy? Did I dream of my pregnancy and the ambulance ride? I was losing it. No one spoke of the stillborn child—my baby. Life went on as if nothing had happened, as if no one died. My abuse of alcohol and prescription drugs escalated. The voices were increasing in frequency and getting louder and louder. I couldn't hear myself think.

I was stuck in the anger stage of grief for many years and did not understand what I was going through. This led to more suicide attempts as well as an incorrect diagnosis by well-meaning physicians. Alcoholism can produce symptoms of all kinds of mental illness.

Hawaiian Beaches

My marriage to David came with some benefits. For example, he worked for the airlines, and we were able to fly anywhere with the only out-of-pocket expense being the tax. Of course, we had to fly on stand-by status, but this was not a problem because David knew a lot of people.

On more than one occasion, I took advantage of that benefit and flew to Hawaii just to get away and relax. I could drink as much as I wanted, and the ocean waves helped drown out the voices. David worked and I went to Hawaii. No wonder there were problems in our marriage.

Hawaii is truly a paradise, but my last trip there was a disaster, and to this day, remains somewhat of a blur. I either slept through most of the trip or passed out from the alcoholic beverages. The flight was long, and the cabin pressure on the plane makes one very thirsty. David and I were already at odds. He traveled extensively, worked long hours, and was frequently absent. I didn't know how to handle the loneliness. I didn't have any girlfriends. However, the voices hadn't deserted me, and alcohol kept me warm and mellow. I should have realized then perhaps I had a drinking problem.

After the plane landed, I took the shuttle bus from the airport in Honolulu to the hotel. I checked in, unpacked, and headed for the beautiful beaches. Instead of taking walks, touring, reading a good book, shopping, or actually resting, I proceeded to drink. Instead of seeing God's handiwork in the beauty of the flowers, the emerald green and sapphire blue waters, the white, sandy beaches, I chose to lie on the beach and drink until I passed out. (I told people I fell asleep.) While "asleep," I got a *very* angry sunburn. Fever and chills were my companions on the flight back to Texas. The airline staff did everything possible to keep me comfortable (after all, I was the wife of one of their own), but I was delirious. I blistered in the worst way.

Did I learn my lesson? Did I see how damaging alcohol can be? Did I see loneliness wasn't resolved by getting drunk? I wish the answer was "yes."

"Turn to me and be gracious to me, for I am
lonely and afflicted."
PSALM 25:16

7

Reunion

ON A MORE positive note, thanks to David's airline benefits, I was able to fly back to Japan in 1970 and reunite with my birth mother, Matsue. I had not seen nor heard from her since the day Helen and Jesse took me away in the big, green car. I was likely pregnant with my son, RC, at the time so he got to go to Japan, too.

After extensive and exhaustive research, with assistance from the Japanese consulate, I located Matsue. She was still living in the same town of Otsu, Japan. With the aid of interpreters, we arranged for David and me to meet my mother at the train station in Kyoto, Japan. Trains and train stations have played important roles in my tumultuous life, wouldn't you agree?

Fifteen years had passed since the last time I was in Kyoto. That's the town where Matsue and I would go for our hot baths, window-shopping trips, and to watch plays at the Kabuki theater. That's where I would see Matsue smile after I indulged in saké and sang and danced for her.

After years of separation, our meeting was surreal. Matsue was dressed in her native kimono. She was not very tall, maybe five feet and two inches. She weighed a hundred pounds at most. Matsue did not speak English, and most of my Japanese was erased, or so I thought. After a few weeks in Japan, many Japanese words and phrases came back to me. However, our conversations were extremely limited, and the reunion didn't lend itself to asking questions about my birth father. Nor did our reunion seem appropriate for me to ask why she relinquished me for adoption. Matsue let us know she had not had any other children.

While on the plane to Japan, my imagination challenged me as several scenarios of what I would say and how our meeting would go danced before my eyes. Would we run into each other's arms? Would I call her "Mother"? Would she lavish me with hugs and kisses?

None of the imagined scenarios happened. We just stared at each other in an awkward silence. Then, slowly, we walked toward each other with apprehension and stiffness. After years of separation and years of unanswered questions, we stood within two feet of each other, face to face, just staring. What will the first move be? Who would make it?

I dropped my luggage and walked that last step to her and embraced her. Matsue embraced me back, and we stood silently in the throng of people, oblivious to our surroundings. We wept and hugged and didn't let go of each other for what seemed like a decade.

The three of us rode in a taxi to the hotel. Matsue suggested we settle in at the hotel and then see the sights. It was amazing how the language of my native country came flooding back. Conversational Japanese was still with me, and I could understand enough to communicate with gestures and a few words.

"*Eriko-san,* you have grown up. You're a young lady now. You have a better life." Matsue said these words over and over again.

"Yes, *Okasan.* You gave me this better life."

It was important to me she knew how her sacrifice had paid off in spades. It was important she knew I didn't feel anger and animosity within me for what she had done: selling me to strangers for a mere two-hundred dollars for adoption fees through the military. She relinquished me for adoption to strangers with hope of a better future for me.

During the time we spent in Japan, the three of us did some sightseeing and visited as much as we could. It was not a time for me to ask questions about my past. It was not a time to ask, "Who is my father?" We let our time be sweet and ended with a promise to keep in touch, which we did.

David and I flew back to the States. Matsue and I kept our promise to write, exchanging many letters that had to be translated from Japanese to English and from English to Japanese.

My most treasured photograph is one I received from Matsue—a photo of the two of us shortly before she relinquished me for adoption.

Pre-Adoption

Reunion

Matsue eventually married, and, for many years, she and her husband were happy. Unfortunately, a tragic auto accident occurred right in front of their house in their seventeenth year of marriage. Her husband died instantly. Matsue then started working in a gift shop on Lake Biwa, where we used to live, until she retired. She had no other children. She eventually had physical problems with her legs and lived her later years in a home, where she was very happy because of the help and medical assistance available to her.

When I found out through the Japanese consulate's office she had died in the 1990s, I cried. I cried for the times we never had. I cried for her visit to the United States that didn't happen.

I had gotten sober before Matsue died, so I truly felt the grief, the sadness, and the loss of what would never be. Thanks to God's mercy, I did not use her death as a reason to grab a drink or take antidepressants. What a miracle to go through grief completely sober.

"Peace I leave with you; my peace I give you. I do not give to you as the world gives. Do not let your hearts be troubled and do not be afraid."
JOHN 14:27

Regrets? I do not have them. Why? Because I know Matsue did the best she could. She loved me, provided for me, and in her way, I think she prayed for me. I am thankful for her selfless sacrifice.

Joy Two

The other joy that came from my marriage to David was the birth of my son, RC. God granted me this precious gift of life. At that time, RC was the only thing in my life that gave me a desire to live. I even saw the moon on occasion, and the voices got quieter. Again, I didn't drink alcohol or abuse pills during my pregnancy because I couldn't. For me, morning sickness was a blessing.

RC was a big baby—truly a bundle of joy. He was ahead in all aspects of infancy. He thoroughly enjoyed playing with pots and pans and empty boxes. He loved being read to, and I loved reading to him.

David traveled with the airlines, so RC and I spent a lot of time together, just mother and son. When the voices started keeping me company again, I would turn to the bottle or to the pills. The voices would say, "What kind of mother are you? You drink. You don't have the money to buy nice things for your son. Your husband's always gone. What kind of life can you give RC? Maybe RC would be better off if you weren't around. David can take better care of him than you can."

Sometimes I would quiet the voices with a rum-and-coke, or Jack Daniels-and-coke, or whatever I could get, and then the voices would just whisper. But the voices were once again a constant in my life again as was the alcohol.

Trouble

Early on in our marriage, David and I had problems. Most of them stemmed from my drinking. Neither of us knew how to handle alcohol, nor did we know how to resolve our differences in a healthy way. We did not know how to communicate. David did what he was able to do, but I was quite a handful.

David had a very good sense of humor and was well-liked. Helen and Jesse liked him a lot. After all, he was a college graduate, had a good job, and told a lot of jokes. *They* thought he was great. Helen would call me on the phone and say, "You're so lucky he married you. Does he know about you? Does he know the past you've had?" I was dumb enough to listen to her. I didn't know I could tell her "Goodbye," and hang up the phone. They never knew about David's character flaws. We all have them, right?

One of my female clients a few years ago relayed an experience I have permission to share because parts of it are parallel and relevant to my journey of recovery.

Candice sat in the chair in front of me with blackened eyes and a swollen lip. She had trouble getting into a comfortable position. Candice was married to a very handsome, educated man who was well-liked by everyone he met. He was personable and knew how to help everyone feel relaxed and at ease.

"Dr. V, my husband was away on a business trip one day. I was so bored and felt all alone. I went out by the pool to get some attention and have a conversation. I had been drinking most of the day and found myself flirting with someone I met in the laundry room of the apartment complex. He was married and told me his wife was out of town. Dr. V, I was so lonely and pretty looped. I had already had several drinks, and it was only three in the afternoon. He asked me to come up to their apartment, and we started making out. That's when my husband Mark surprised us by coming home early due to equipment problems at work. Enraged, Mark stormed into his friend's apartment to ask him if he had seen me. Mark found his friend and me making out. I was so ashamed, Dr. V. I knew what I was doing was wrong. I ran out of the man's apartment back to ours. My husband found me huddled in a corner, whimpering. He started calling me awful names, and I just sat there, not saying a word. Everything he said was true. Then, he grabbed me by my hair and started punching me. I fell and hit my head on something hard. Dr. V, I deserved every punch he hurled. I deserved the black eye and swollen jaw. If Mark hadn't found me making out with this man when he did, who knows what we would have ended up doing. Yes, I deserved to be beaten."

As Candice shared her experience with me, I prayed God would give me the guidance to help her. Therapists know not to give advice, but during times of danger, we provide names of local shelters and assist in any way we can to get our clients to a safe environment. We are trained to report abuse to the proper authorities.

Under no circumstance is it okay for a man or a woman to hurt you physically, especially while they are in the midst of anger. No matter what you've done, it is *not okay* to be struck and beaten by your husband or wife, boyfriend or girlfriend, or anyone else. Go to a shelter or get some help from a trusted friend or from your church. Run as fast as you can from any physical violence. You are a child of God and not a vehicle for someone to inflict anger through physical pain. Even if the physical violence feels familiar to you, run from it.

I remember when I experienced a similar situation while married to David, and actually sought counseling to find out why I drank and flirted so much. I checked with various agencies that promoted "affordable" counseling. I selected a very well-known agency, because I was afraid to use our health insurance benefits for fear David would find out. After weeks of vacillating back and forth, I made the call. "Hi. I need counseling. How much do you charge?" It took a tremendous amount of courage for me to make this call. Unfortunately, for me and for everyone affected by my behavior, this agency would not accept me, because we exceeded the income level by twenty-eight dollars to qualify for their "affordable" counseling. So much for that. I needed an excuse to *not* get help, and, by golly, here it was.

I see today God did not want me to waste the hurt. Perhaps, this is one of the reasons why our organization is so liberal with our sliding scale fee structure. No one should be turned away if they want professional counseling, even if they can't afford to pay. I thank God for allowing me to have this experience of being turned down.

My self-esteem was still very low, yet something inside me told me I did not deserve the physical violence from David. I had put up with it from Jesse, but I was *not* going to put up with it any longer from *anyone.* I took RC, who was still a toddler, and left.

I immediately got a job at a local restaurant. The manager was kind and hired me even with physical evidence of a recent altercation with David. Bob helped us get on our feet. He would later become husband number two.

Bob and I were married shortly after my divorce from David. Bob took really good care of us and loved RC like his own son. He was a good man and a hard worker. Sadly, I still didn't know how to handle loneliness. All I knew was how to drink the loneliness away or take tranquilizers to chill me out. The restaurant business involves long hours, and Bob often did not come home until after two in the morning. He was just trying to provide for his family, but once again my drinking and prescription drug addiction took its toll.

I was hearing voices at an accelerated pace, and each voice screamed to be heard. I didn't realize there was an intense spiritual war going on, a battle for my very existence. It appeared the voices were winning. Each voice had specific things to say.

"You're worthless!" one would yell.

"What a tramp you are!" another would shout.

"Your son deserves a better mother, don't you think?" asked one in a shrill voice, cruelly mocking me. Each distinct voice would take a turn, hurling obscenities and condemnation.

"Bob deserves a better wife." The voices were intimately aware of everything about me. Soon, the voices took their place and gained control once again. I stopped looking for the moon and knew the only relief was permanent escape.

One day, Bob left for work after his break between shifts. He worked many long hours and wouldn't be home for a long time. This was the perfect time. *Now!* He wouldn't be home until after two in the morning, and it was only four-thirty in the afternoon. I would be long gone by the time he came home. I took my son to a neighbor's apartment and told her I was going to take a nap.

A bottle of tranquillizers was in my possession, and I swallowed all of them with whatever bottle of booze we happened to have at the apartment. I lay down to go to sleep, forever. There was no dog to bounce on my bed. No moon in the night. No voices in my head. Bob would not be home for hours. No way will this get fouled up this time. This time, I'm doing it right.

As luck, fate, coincidence, or my favorite, God, would have it, Bob had forgotten his liquor cabinet keys and had to return to the apartment. He found me unconscious but still alive and took me to a hospital. They pumped my stomach, and I had to be evaluated by a psychiatrist. The doctor determined I was manic-depressive (now known as bipolar) and gave me medication. I had to promise I would follow up as an outpatient with a psychiatrist as part of the requirements for release from the hospital.

Prescribing antidepressants for me was again just what I needed—more pills. Have you ever taken the time to read all the fine print on television ads? Phrases like, "Your depression may worsen," or "Thoughts of suicide may increase." I know physicians weigh the risks and the benefits, but for someone who drinks depressants (alcohol) and had attempted suicide several times, another alternative might have been better.

"Do you drink?" the doctor asked.

"Only socially," I said. "An occasional glass of wine or two." Of course, I would lie to the well-meaning psychiatrist about my drinking. It wasn't his fault. I know the doctor meant well. And, of course, I didn't follow up as directed. I didn't return for any more follow-up appointments. Naturally, I continued to drink.

Assessments and tests do not always reveal the truth. Patients know how to manipulate the answers—I sure did—and will mark answers they want to be seen which are not necessarily the truth. Doctors can only go by what we tell them, and as a result, are not always able to get to the cause. It helps to tell the truth.

I've often wondered what the role of psychiatrists would be if they did not prescribe medication. I've heard it said, "If you go to a barbershop, you'll end up with a haircut sooner or later." I believe this philosophy also applies to psychiatrists. If you see a psychiatrist, you'll end up with a label and some medication based on what you report, which is not necessarily the truth. This is just my opinion. Even with my lies, or maybe because of them, I was given three different diagnoses the psychiatrist could bill: borderline schizophrenia, multiple personality disorder, and manic-depression. Wow! It was a paperwork fight to get those diagnoses removed years later. It all stemmed from alcohol and prescription drug addiction and unresolved post-traumatic stress. The insanity I struggled with was not any of those labels given. I just didn't know this at the time.

Bob and I were married for ten years. During that time, we had a daughter, Heather. She was, and still is, my sunshine. She is also the apple of her daddy's eye. Bob was patient, hardworking, and loyal. I, on the other hand, went out to clubs and went out of town with my friend Nancy who was single. She and I would spend weekends away, drinking, partying, and having the time of our lives while Bob was home with RC and Heather.

Nancy and I are still friends today. By God's grace, even though our lives took different paths, we've managed to remain close. She was the follower, and I was the leader. If I drank, she did, too, only not to the extent that I did. She drank socially, without acting stupid or getting intoxicated. She drank normally. I met Nancy at the apartments in 1974, shortly after Bob and I married. She was sunbathing outside by the pool, and I walked up and introduced myself. "Hi. My name is Nancy."

She replied, "Hi, *my* name is Nancy." We've been best friends ever since, through a lot of good times, sad times, and risky times. I'm so grateful my drinking didn't destroy this treasured friendship like it destroyed so many other relationships.

Currently, Nancy, a nonsmoker, is fighting the battle against lung cancer. I ask for your prayers for complete healing.

"A friend loves at all times, and a brother
is born for a time of adversity."
PROVERBS 17:17

8

"Whether-related"

DRINKING AND DRIVING is a dangerous and senseless thing to do. I had five car wrecks during my marriages to David and Bob. Each time, my vehicle was totaled. Each time, God's grace spared me from injuring or killing myself or someone else. No other vehicles were involved in the accidents. The accidents were all "whether-related"...whether I was drinking or not.

According to Mothers Against Drunk Driving (MADD), in 2013, 10,007 people died in drunk-driving crashes in America—twenty-eight people every day. In addition, one person is injured from an alcohol-related crash every minute (www.madd.org/statistics).

On one occasion, I hit a utility pole while going in excess of 110 miles per hour. I was told the impact knocked out the electricity of an entire subdivision. My car was absolutely totaled, and I was unconscious for a period of time. I had a death wish, and, therefore, lived dangerously. Alcohol gave me a false sense of courage. Alcohol was my liquid courage, my social lubricant, and my friend. It is only by the grace of God I survived. Sadly, I was angry I did.

I wasn't always alone when I drove drunk. My daughter, Heather, recalls the following: "You were driving us to church, and we happened to be on the wrong side of the road. I think we did a one-eighty, but no harm, no foul, and no totaling of vehicles, which was something that happened more often then. I can't remember how many car wrecks you were in, but I know there *is* a God, and because of your will and His love and grace, you are still here."

Truly, alcoholism is indeed a horrible addiction that kills the body, mind, and spirit. Because of God's mercy and compassion, I have the desire to stay clean and sober today.

> *"It does not, therefore, depend on human desire or*
> *effort, but on God's mercy."*
> ROMANS 9:16

Better Job

God saw fit to provide me with better employment. I left the food and beverage world in which Bob worked, and I was given a big break in the professional world. Alcohol fueled my ambitions. I literally made cold calls, pounding the streets by walking from one business to another in a nearby business park. God gifted me with abilities and determination I had not yet begun to appreciate. I was hired as an expeditor for an oil and gas company and was successful at what I did: purchasing and logistics.

Several years later, after a layoff, I landed a job at a place called Gateway Technology. I was employee number thirty-one. That company is better known as Compaq Computer Corporation. After years of success, Compaq was purchased by Hewlett-Packard.

Dumper

After ten years of marriage, I decided enough was enough. I realized how unfair I was to Bob, and told him I wanted a divorce. I was the "dumper," because as hard as I tried, he would not leave me. It was very traumatic on our children who suffered greatly not only from this divorce, but also from my abuse of alcohol and prescription drugs. Bob mercifully granted the divorce.

During the years of being single, I acted like an immature, irresponsible teenager. Yet, God's grace was with me. He never left me. I just didn't feel His presence, nor did I have a relationship with Jesus Christ. I continued to drink, party, and act irresponsibly. The alcohol ruled, keeping the voices at bay.

The General

I left Compaq shortly after they went public, and investors encouraged me to join another start-up company. It is there Randall and I met, and we later married. By then, I had incurred the nickname of "The General" in the professional world. Demanding, arrogant, and controlling, I was downright rude to my suppliers, taking advantage of being the one to make purchasing decisions. "You'd better have those parts here by four o'clock tomorrow, or I'll void the contract." Can you imagine someone who is barely five feet tall and weighs ninety-eight pounds being called "The General"? I'm not proud of who I used to be.

Randall and I had our first date on June 17, 1986. We adamantly told each other all the reasons why we would never remarry ever again. He, too, was divorced, and both of us were convinced marriage was for other people.

In September of the same year, he and I were married! Even though I was very active in my alcoholism, I knew he was the one for me. His humility, love of fishing, and love of cooking convinced me. For some reason, knowing he was a Christian was important to me. One of our earlier dates involved going fishing off the Freeport Jetties. A fisherman to my rescue! This felt so familiar. My excessive consumption of alcohol kept the voices fairly quiet. In addition, I felt in charge. I felt in control. Randall helped me feel accepted and loved. I actually thought I was finally learning how to accept love from others. I was wrong.

Blended

Randall and I, his daughter, JR, who was five; and my two children, who were ten and fourteen, became a blended family. Our marriage was challenged in every conceivable way. Children, "friends" who didn't want our marriage to work, my drinking problem, ex-spouses who did not cooperate, and all the baggage I had been carrying around for thirty-six years presented challenges.

Here are some statistics from *Psychology Today*: "Past statistics have shown that in the US, 50% of first marriages, 67% of second, and 73% of third marriages end in divorce. What are the reasons for this progressive increase in divorce rates? Theories abound. One common explanation is that a significant number of people enter a second marriage 'on the rebound' of a first or second divorce. Often the people concerned are vulnerable; they do not allow sufficient time to recover from their divorce, or to get their priorities straight before taking their vows again. They enter their next marriage for the wrong reasons, not having internalized the lessons of their past experience. They are liable to repeat their mistakes." (http://www.psychologytoday.com/blog/the-intelligent-divorce/201202.)

Step It Up
Neither Randall nor I had ever been a step parent, and I can tell you we both made a lot of mistakes. I hope now our children are grown, there is grace and forgiveness. In all likelihood, we will continue to muddle in each phase of life we go through. But I will muddle through them with God's Word and without alcohol or other mind-altering chemicals.

Now our children are adults and life has come full circle. My son has a beautiful family. He and his wife are doing an outstanding job providing for their children in many ways, encouraging the development of their talents, and providing opportunities many children will never have. They are truly blessed. I pray they know how blessed they are and from whom those blessings flow.

My stepdaughter is learning to come to grips with the reality that we have choices in life, and with those choices, come consequences. It took me many years to learn that lesson, so I continue to keep JR in prayer.

Heather is a mature woman, yet young at heart, who knows how to love, share, and laugh. She truly is my most beautiful sunshine. She, too, has had challenges with maintaining marital relationships, and sometimes, I think it's my fault. Then, I remember it's not always about me. All of us face consequences. I just want my children to know joy and to love God. Today, Heather is happily married, and she and her husband, Bill, seem to bring out the best in each other.

Our children have seen firsthand "what it was like, what happened, and what it's like now" (*Big Book, Alcoholics Anonymous, Chapter Five, Third Edition*). All three of our children have made dangerous choices, just as I have, and often still do. They each have a story, but none are mine to tell.

Boundaries

Boundaries are difficult to establish, even more so when you are a stepparent. Because of my drinking and prescription drug abuse, I very rarely meant what I said or said what I meant. Very rarely did I help teach boundaries in our home. I was not a good example for our children. To have boundaries in your family, it's vital to model boundaries in your life. That's hard to do when alcohol controls you.

Without going into too many details, here are some of the mistakes I made: being too permissive, being too strict, not being involved enough with my children's activities, being too involved, saying "yes" too often, saying "no" when I would later change my mind, and trying to be a friend instead of a parent. I lacked consistency. Because of my lack of boundaries, our children had to learn the hard way about establishing their own sense of boundaries. Sometimes, when they practice expressing their boundaries with me, their words are hurtful. But then I have to remember from whence they came.

The best way to teach ourselves and our children a sense of boundaries is God's way. The more I study His word, the more He makes it clear what He expects of me. Thank God I was not and am not the only influence in the lives of our children. Once again, it's not always about me.

I have made choices that held painful consequences. Our children are doing that, too. The good news is they are watching Randall and me, and they continue to see how God works through our pain to draw us closer to Him.

A New Life

Randall and I were married for five years before I took the plunge into sobriety. Prior to this decision, my battle with alcohol—clearly by now my drug of choice—took its toll on our family. My raging, screaming, and verbally abusive behavior toward Randall gave him plenty of justification to leave me. Sometimes, the abuse I inflicted was physical toward him. I truly don't know how he endured.

The bad days outnumbered the good days during our first five years of marriage. My explosive rages got out of control, especially after a few margaritas. I smashed china, dishes, and anything breakable. I didn't realize it at the time, but I was the most broken of all.

Randall would not leave no matter what I did. Once again, the all-too-familiar feelings of shame, guilt, and worthlessness engulfed me. Finally, when I was alone, I came to the realization I might have a problem with alcohol. Duh! Everyone else seemed to know.

One day, while I was at a gathering, I heard Cheryl, one of the women guests, talk about how abusive her husband was toward her. With her rivulet of tears, she shared her story: "Whenever my husband drank, he would scream at me and pick fights over the slightest of differences. He would get enraged and start tearing up our house by smashing and throwing things—even things he prized. If I even glanced at another male, he would automatically think something was going on, and make accusations that were so untrue."

It took hearing someone else describe the pain they felt when abuse was dished out to them to see the harm I was causing to others. Through her words and through her pain, I finally saw myself and the torment I was inflicting on my family.

One Sunday, I sat in the parking lot wanting so badly to go to church. I knew that was where the answers were. I knew that was where I belonged. I felt such emptiness and a longing. The Bible class was something I usually looked forward to, and the church choir was a big part of my life. But all I could do was sit in my car in the parking lot next door and cry. My feelings of self-loathing wouldn't permit me to even park in the church parking lot. I didn't make it inside that day. Of course, I had already had a few drinks. I wanted to smile and needed desperately to belong. I ached for peace and longed for joy.

On September 28, 1991, I was invited to attend a recovery program for alcoholics in support of someone very close to me. As I sat there, supporting my friend, I heard the main speaker describe the car wrecks he had been involved in. Bruce said, "I had an empty void. There was no joy, only pain." I understood the empty void he described. He said, "I didn't like who I had become. I'd be in a crowded room, and, yet, I felt all alone. The only friends I had weren't friends at all. They were just people to drink with." As he described the isolation he experienced, I saw myself. "I never fit in, and didn't feel like I belonged anywhere. I felt as if I were an outcast, a leper." How was he able to look inside of me? How did he know the thoughts and emotions I was experiencing?

To me, this was a little strange, because he never spoke a word about being adopted. All of my life, I used adoption as the excuse for why I was so messed up. Maybe the fact I was adopted had nothing to do with why I felt so isolated. Is that even possible?

Bruce continued, "My life had become unmanageable, and I was a mess." The speaker was describing me. How could that be? I knew at that moment if *his* life was a mess, so was *mine*. I was powerless over alcohol. I knew *my* life had indeed become unmanageable.

Interestingly enough, this is Step One of the Twelve Steps of Alcoholics Anonymous: "We admitted we were powerless over alcohol and our lives had become unmanageable." The scriptural reference is as follows: "For I know that good itself does not dwell in me, that is, in my sinful nature. For I have the desire to do what good, but I cannot carry it out." (Romans 7:18.)

At the end of Bruce's talk, there was an invitation of sorts to come forward and publicly acknowledge being powerless over alcohol, and to accept an outward token of an inward desire to stay sober, one day at a time.

Although I tried to remain in my seat at the back of the room, it was as if a force much stronger than anything I've ever experienced pushed me out of my chair toward the front of the room. Even though I wanted to sit back down, there was another force pulling me toward the front.

I know you may think this sounds really hokey, but I believe this was a spiritual experience. It was then and there I made my decision in front of a roomful of witnesses to surrender my alcoholism and my life to God's care.

"Do you have any idea what you've done? Do you know what this means?" My husband of five years begged for answers from me. On September 28, 1991, I didn't have a clue.

I know there are many people who are not in favor of Twelve Step programs, but I, for one, am grateful, because this program, through God's grace, saved my life...in more ways than one. Did my decision to stop drinking and lead a sober life make everything easy? Did it mean that my life now would be a piece of cake? Far from it! This was the beginning of a new way of living, and I didn't have a clue how to do life sober.

"I can do all this through him who gives me strength."
PHILIPPIANS 4:13

9

Revenge is Mine!

AFTER BEING WITHOUT alcohol or antidepressants for about six weeks, my mind became clearer, and I started having what are known as flashbacks. The images in my mind's eye were very vivid. They were both frightening and disgusting. I saw images of me when I was a young child living with Matsue, and with Helen and Jesse, images of molestation from different men, and flashbacks of the rapes. The pictures through my mind's eye were so clear it made it impossible for me to have sex with my husband.

For what it's worth, Randall was very patient and kind. There were a few times he would find me hiding in the closet, curled up in a fetal position. "What are you doing?" he would ask. All I could do was cry. He got literature on my condition, and read up on how spouses can help survivors of incest. He remained faithful even when I tried to get him to hate me. I would have mood swings and death wishes, hoping and praying that an eighteen-wheeler would run me down, or that a tree limb would fall off a large oak tree and hit my head, killing me. Without alcohol, the voices were speaking out loudly and with a vengeance to drink, to hurt someone, and to die.

"I want to hurt Helen and Jesse for all the pain they caused me. I want them to die!" Randall heard it all. He listened and witnessed my anger and my hatred for them and for Matsue. As Matsue lived in another country, and Helen and Jesse were more accessible, Helen and Jesse became my target. I was determined to seek revenge any way I could. "I want to get a gun and shoot them," I would say. "God, I need help!"

Randall and I had a thorough discussion. We were in agreement I desperately needed professional help. I knew seeking revenge was not the way to live a sober life. I knew this was not part of God's plan for me: to hurt someone and possibly end up in prison for the actions I desperately wanted to take. In all honesty, I didn't want to inflict pain on others any more than I already had. I was fighting the urge to get on the next flight to Washington and take a life. If the decision to get help was not acted upon, there was no telling what would have transpired. God protected me from the "what if's" once again.

After researching several options, we found a hospital and I was checked in for an intensive ten-day stay. This particular hospital had a program of regression therapy. Regression therapy is somewhat controversial and not for everyone. In my case, it was very beneficial. It helped me to see with clarity that which was so close to the surface. It helped me to reclaim a childhood lost.

Here's a brief overview of regression therapy:

"The three levels of consciousness that are recognized in regression therapy include: The conscious mind, representing what a person does; the sub-conscious mind, representing what a person is; and the super-conscious mind, also known as the spirit. Regression therapy is built on the foundation that people are born with a distinct set of emotions and definitive personality. Life experiences alter and reinforce those fundamentals in such a manner that they become part of our psychological blueprint. If the emotion is a negative one, it will eventually emerge in our adult life in the form of symptomatic behaviors or relational challenges." (http://www.goodtherapy.org/regression-therapy.html.)

Through these ten exhausting days, I came to understand Matsue was just trying to survive the only way she knew how. The therapy allowed me to walk through the entirety of the flashbacks and receive affirmation I had survived. Memories cannot harm me. I am safe. I understood how very ill Helen truly was. She had survived a terrible war and was even imprisoned in a concentration camp. She had witnessed so much death. I saw clearly Jesse didn't know any other way to discipline. Cursing, yelling, and whipping me was all he knew because that is how he grew up.

Play Time!

Part of my therapy was learning how to play and have fun. As a child, I didn't know what fun was, nor did I know how to achieve it. Experiencing the joys of childhood was foreign to me. I had experienced so much adulthood at such a young age, I missed out completely on the joys of just being a kid.

One day, while we were in the cafeteria, I had the urge to participate in a food fight. (I had seen something on TV, and I remembered laughing about it.) So, I looked around and found someone I believed to be a safe target. It happened to be the resident psychiatrist, of all people. I looked at my table-setting and saw a dish of wiggly, squiggly, red Jell-O. I actually had the courage to fling the Jell-O across the table and hit my mark!

There was a moment of silence. The entire room suddenly became as quiet as a bale of cotton. All of a sudden, the psychiatrist stood up, all six-feet-four inches of him. We were holding our breath and didn't know what his reaction would be. He looked down at the table before him, and then slowly lifted his steel-gray eyes and looked right at me with a piercing glare. Maybe I was wrong. Maybe he wasn't safe after all. Maybe all this talk about reclaiming your childhood was just that: talk.

Suddenly, out of nowhere came a big glob of Jell-O, plopping down right on our table. What occurred next could have made an interesting episode for the *Three Stooges*. Several others got in on the action, and there was Jell-O flying everywhere. An explosion of laughter and clapping erupted. After we cleaned up the mess, the resident psychiatrist came over and said, "Congratulations. You're learning to live."

A few days after the food fight experience, my group went on an outing. Guess where we went? Toys "R" Us! It never occurred to me as an adult I could actually buy something fun just for me. My children had games, stuffed animals, and books purchased for their pleasure and enjoyment. The extent of my toy collection as a child consisted of a rag-doll named Mary, a teddy bear I called Cookie, a Barbie doll I hated because she was so perfect, and a Monopoly set with some missing pieces. That was it. So a trip to Toys "R" Us was indeed a very special event.

In grocery stores, I always envied the small children whose mom or dad pushed them around in their shopping carts. I pushed my own children in the carts when they were toddlers, and I would envy them, too. While I was at the toy store on our outing, I expressed this to one of the counselors. Guess what happened next? I ended up in the shopping cart! The counselor pushed me up and down each aisle until I was delirious with laughter. It's such a small thing and absolutely ridiculous to imagine, but this was yet another opportunity to experience being a kid. I wasn't even embarrassed other shoppers saw this adult woman being pushed around like a child in a shopping cart. I wonder how many of them were jealous. I was learning to laugh and learning to have fun. I was learning to not be self-conscious—indeed, learning how to start living.

When my ten-day stay at the hospital ended and I came home, Randall had stocked up on board games. I think he bought out whatever store he went to! Puzzles, games, and a set of jacks—all for me! One of the puzzles was of Mickey and Minnie Mouse. He and I put it together, and to this day, it is intact, framed, and hanging in my home office. I still have the jacks, and a stuffed animal called "Southern Comfort" sits proudly on the bed in our guest bedroom. Randall's gestures of thoughtfulness and loving kindness will stay with me always.

My family was, and still is, so supportive, especially my husband. He had every reason in the world to leave me. I was an abusive alcoholic and a horrible housekeeper to boot. I didn't even cook. By the way, I still do very little cooking. If Randall doesn't cook, we go out! He is amazing. My family allowed me to be young again. I learned how to play games (without cheating), put together puzzles, laugh, and have fun.

Another aspect of marriage had to be learned. I had never had sex sober. The flashbacks were so difficult to walk through. Randall was patient with me when I could not stand to be touched, and when I would cringe at the thought of intimacy. As I said earlier, he had every reason to leave me. Yet, he was faithful, supportive, and understanding. I am so grateful for his support and the support of my family. They may not have understood what I was working through, but they supported me nonetheless.

My new way of life—being sober and sober-minded—was different not just for me, but also for my family and my friends. For our three children, this meant all of a sudden rules had to be followed. It meant suddenly there were consequences to skipping school, stealing, lying, etc. It's really a miracle my children even speak to me, after what they had to endure through my alcoholism. All three children, now grown, have their own stories to share.

Through God's grace, we survived the harried years with the challenges of a blended family, and the complications of preteen/teenage hormones, and an alcoholic in recovery.

I hope and pray the changes that have been and continue to be made show our adult children there is hope for a better life. I pray they are watching our lives and see His miracles unfold.

Sobering Moments

My first New Year's Eve party in sobriety was an unforgettable experience. It was held at our Twelve Step meeting place in Tomball, Texas. This was a family affair. My newly made friends were there and so were my husband and both daughters. This should have been a great way to ring in the New Year, right?

Well, what fun I had—*not!* The children were dancing and eating the potluck food (there was so much of it), and my husband and I were seated at a table. I had my arms crossed. If the lights weren't so low, you would have seen the scowl on my face and my clenched jaws and fists. How *dare* they. Everyone was laughing, dancing, wearing party hats, and having fun. *You call this fun?* I thought. How can you have fun without alcohol? I've had all the coffee I can stand. See what I mean about learning to live life sober? I really didn't have a clue.

After about an hour of this so-called "fun," I'd had enough. I stormed out, got in my car, left my family, and took off for home. I guess by the time I got to our house I had calmed down somewhat. Just because I had gotten sober did not mean I became a nice person. I was still very self-centered and selfish. It was all about me and what I wanted.

A friend of mine explained to me what I was going through was a stage of grief. I was angry at God for letting me be an alcoholic. I was angry I couldn't drink, even on New Year's Eve! How bad could one drink to bring in the New Year be? My family came home shortly thereafter, and I was feeling pretty rotten about my behavior.

Some of the other holiday firsts were also challenging. Nonetheless, God's grace reminded me to rely on Him and the people in recovery whom He put in my life.

> *"Be alert and of sober mind.*
> *Your enemy the devil prowls around*
> *like a roaring lion looking for*
> *someone to devour."*
> FIRST PETER 5:8

When Helen died, I had been sober for five months. I had to get to Washington quickly, which meant it was necessary to catch a plane and fly. This was not good. Flying had always been a major trigger for me to drink. (Well, truth be known, a flat tire, a rainy day, a hot day, weddings, etc., were all triggers for me.) My career in logistics and purchasing required a lot of traveling, so I drank a lot.

What I had to do was take recovery literature, and, of course, the Bible with me on the airplane. The airline hostess during the long flight would often walk by with her cheery smile and offer alcoholic beverages. My prayer life grew immensely. *God, help me stay sober. God, keep me from drinking.* He did. God's grace was so evident on that trip.

When I landed in Washington and got to the hotel, guess what was within walking distance: A place that held AA meetings several times throughout the day, every day of the week. It was like going to church every day—hearing spiritual messages, praying before and after each meeting, hugging, and exchanging phone numbers with other women in recovery for support.

The day of the memorial service, several women came to Jesse's house and brought food. They even brought me clothes to wear because I had forgotten appropriate clothing. Mind you, these women were complete strangers, except for a few meetings together. They were such a support to my family and me. Many of the women stayed to attend the service. Yes, these women were strangers, but they knew me well. They understood how easy it would have been to pick up that first drink.

From the acts of kindness from strangers, I learned the importance of giving to others in need. I learned the value of extending a hand and your heart to others in pain. God put those women in my life for a very specific reason. These strangers walked with me through a very painful and confusing time. For that, I am eternally grateful.

Now, of course, deaths, births, and other special occasions don't present a problem for me. I understand yours truly cannot have a drink. I cannot play Russian roulette with alcohol because drinking could destroy me. It could also destroy everything God has so mercifully given me. So, for today, having that first drink after twenty-three years of sober living is not an option for me. Today, God has allowed me to choose not to drink.

Another Wife?

Not too long after Helen died, it was laid on my heart to take back my birth name. Randall once again was supportive. He had known me for five years as his wife named Nancy. So, when I announced I wanted to reclaim my birth name, Eriko, he never batted an eye. My name change was done through the court system. After being fingerprinted—only four times—and providing required documents of my birth registration and adoption papers, I went before a judge once again.

"Why do you want to change your name?" asked the judge.

"Your Honor, I'm really not changing my name; I'm reclaiming my birth name." After a few questions, he ordered the courts to acknowledge my first name officially as Eriko. The correct pronunciation is "ehdiko." The "d" sounds like a soft rolled "r." In Japan, Eriko is a very common name that means "logic" or "reason." I kept "Nancy" as my middle name. One could say my names mean "logically graceful." Or not.

Randall's mother, Nellie—who I loved dearly and is now deceased and with the Lord—told us a very funny story shortly after my name change. She loved to gab on the phone for hours. One of her friends said, "I called Randy, and the answering machine came on with the strangest message. It said, 'You have reached Randy and Eriko. We're unavailable right now, so please leave a message after the beep.' Who is Eriko? I thought his wife's name is Nancy. Did Randy get remarried *again*?" Everyone had a good laugh about that. Nellie was such a great sport about it. I know it caused quite a stir in her circle of friends that Nellie and Bob's son got married...again.

My son said the following about my name change: "The whole thing about the name change, I don't get it." It is my hope he chooses to read this, and it is my prayer he will then understand. Besides, my children never called me anything else other than "Mom." I will always be their mom, no matter what, and I hope to be the best mom I am able to be, through His grace.

MOM!

"MOM! MOM!" My children would call for me. I didn't know they were screaming. After we were married only a few weeks, Randall was horrified. He would ask, "Why are your children yelling at you?"

"They're not yelling; they're just calling for me," I would reply. Turns out they indeed were yelling, not because they were being disrespectful (most of the time), but because I wasn't hearing them unless they did. Neither I nor my children really understood the depth of my hearing loss.

After several ear infections, it was time for yet another major ear operation. It was very traumatic for me after the recovery and the bandages came off. For the first time in my life, I was able to hear trucks on the freeway. For the first time in my life, I heard the sound of a toilet flushing. All these new strange sounds created anxiety, frustration, and tears, because I didn't know how to handle the noise. What were normal everyday sounds to others frightened me. At home, everyone had to walk on tiptoes, literally. In fact, putting away dishes and silverware was such a nerve-racking experience I would cry from the pain of the sounds. Learning to identify what dishes sound like when placed on top of one another, and identifying the clanking of silverware in a drawer, was all new to me.

I was not yet sober at this time, so I was still coping with the help of alcohol instead of leaning on God. Thankfully, my husband was so patient, and my children were as understanding as children are capable of being.

The otolaryngologist told us, "Nancy has about five more years of hearing left. (This was in 1988.) It will slowly disintegrate, and she will be completely deaf. I suggest she learn American Sign Language (ASL)." I refused. I was not going to be deaf.

"I found this online and thought it would help you learn ASL," my husband told me. The set of VCR tapes (DVDs were not available yet) arrived. I may have viewed them once. Okay, maybe twice. I cried. It was awful to think I was going to have to "hear" people talk with their hands. I just couldn't do it and refused to learn. I did not want to be "handi-capped." We put the tapes on a top shelf where they collected dust for many years. We moved them from house to house until we finally gave them away to someone who *wanted* to learn sign language. I'm grateful they were put to good use, because I was not going to learn ASL.

The doctors were right. My hearing did deteriorate slowly. But I did not go completely deaf for many years after their prediction. God granted me so many years of limited hearing so my lip-reading skills could be perfected, without me even realizing this was happening. I thank Him for this.

> *"It was good for me to be afflicted so that*
> *I might learn your decrees."*
> PSALM 119:71

Yes, I Will Be Your Friend

Sobriety meant changes in my circle of friends. My career path changed direction (Hello, God), and I was blessed to have a chance to work with a school district as a para-professional for several years. During the course of those years, many dear female friends were made, and we keep in touch even today. We've gone on trips together, and we have lunch and share times of laughter and tears. I cannot be more grateful for the support I received not only from my church and my recovery and support groups, but also from the women of the elementary school who allowed me to be imperfect and loved me anyway. My friends Shirley and Lee Ann are there for me to this day, and I know they always will be.

Meanwhile my husband and I became active in a smaller local church and got involved in various ministries. The women in our Bible study group are so precious. They are real. Sometimes it was difficult for me to be open. It was hard for me to talk about wanting to drink during Bible study. It wasn't them; it was me. So I continued to combine my recovery support groups with church attendance. It was a good fit for me.

Little Red Schoolhouse Two

After my job as a para-professional, I gained employment within an organization that provides housing, life-skills training, and job opportunities to adults who are challenged mentally. This was the beginning of a new path for me. This was the groundwork for a vision that was birthed. I saw the need for family members of these special adults who needed guidance, support, and counseling. They struggled with financial burdens, stress, and marital discord. Somehow, I think the experience I had as a child in that "Little Red Schoolhouse" fueled my passion to help adults who are mentally challenged. What if I had not had that experience? God knew what my future held. He had a plan for me.

> "Many are the plans in a person's heart,
> but it is the Lord's purpose that prevails."
> PROVERBS 19:21

10

Double Doc

In 2004, I completed all the requirements for receiving my doctorate degrees in social work and in psychology. My husband was ecstatic. We talked about him retiring and my having a small private practice, seeing a handful of clients, and both of us spending most days fishing offshore. God had other plans.

I can't explain how or why, but the burden of providing a place where parents, individuals, and families could come for counseling, even if they couldn't afford to pay, was prominent in my heart and mind. I'm sure the memory of being turned down by that large agency years ago because I made "too much money" had some bearing on this. What if?

Randall at first was rather disappointed (actually, I thought he was going to cry) and questioned my sanity. So did I. "Are you crazy? You want to start a nonprofit? You're nuts!" he exclaimed. Since that brief moment of doubt, Randall has been our greatest supporter in every way.

Our founding board of five directors pulled together three-thousand dollars, and after much prayer, work, and more prayer, we started Liberty Path, Inc. Liberty Path is a nonprofit public charity that provides professional, Christian-based counseling, regardless of one's ability to pay. Families with special-needs children always receive our services at no cost. Period. Our church was gracious and allowed us to use one of their rooms when we first opened for business. Then, after much research on office space, we found a more permanent solution. With a huge step of faith, we signed a lease for office space. We had nothing to rely on except for God's grace for provisions—no donation base, no major funding, no grant monies, zilch. Just God.

Many miracles have occurred. So many times God has showed His hand is upon us. For example, our first of five office spaces had 469 square feet. Our rent cost about seven-hundred dollars at that time, but we only had about thirty. However, we had such a peace. No panic, no stress. I closed our checkbook, walked to the mailbox, and inside the mailbox was a check for four-thousand dollars. The donation came from a neighbor of a young man for whom we were providing counseling at no charge. We were able to pay rent and the rest of our bills for a few months.

Thankfully, God has shown His favor throughout the life of our ministry for which I am truly grateful.

> *"But he said to me, 'My grace is sufficient for you,*
> *for my power is made perfect in weakness.'*
> *Therefore I will boast all the more gladly about my*
> *weaknesses, so that Christ's power may rest on me."*
> SECOND CORINTHIANS *12:9*

Slipping

To help promote our organization, I joined several professional networking groups. One of them was Northwest Houston Business and Professional Women, or Northwest Houston BPW.

On the morning of our luncheon, the button on my skirt popped off. As I was running late for work, I used a safety pin for a fast remedy. With an armful of binders and presentation materials, I walked through the venue parking lot. Unfortunately, the safety pin popped off, and my skirt came down around my ankles! There happened to be an eighteen-wheeler with its engine running in the parking lot at that very moment, delivering linens. I'm not sure if anyone saw this embarrassing moment or not. I didn't dare turn around to see.

What could I do? I set my binders down, pulled up my skirt, refastened the safety pin, gathered my belongings, and walked into the meeting place. I was so filled with gratitude that day. I was thankful I did not find it necessary to drink over my dilemma. In fact, I was asked to lead our invocation. I chose to talk about gratitude...gratitude that even if my skirt fell down, I was able to be thankful I had on a slip.

Professional Networking

After my "slip-up," there were several women who came up and spoke to me. I was very shy (self-conscious) and nervous about making friends. For so long, I had not trusted women. By sharing about my slip-up, I allowed them to see I was vulnerable. I allowed these professional women, most of whom I did not know, to see me as a human being with flaws, blemishes, and imperfections. Before, I needed alcohol as my "social lubricant." Leaning on God gave me the courage to replace the liquid courage that used to be my crutch. Many of these precious ladies have become dear, longtime friends. In fact, several of them have taken terms serving on our board.

As a group, Northwest Houston BPW has donated financial gifts, much-needed office supplies, and gifts-in-kind (gift cards for our clients) to Liberty Path. In addition, they refer their friends to our agency and show their support by attending our fundraisers. We are so grateful for all they do to assist us.

My friend Mary belongs to another professional group called Women's Business Forum (WBF). Thanks to her input, WBF has selected Liberty Path to be the beneficiary of their fundraisers on several occasions. I'm amazed what this small group (by choice) of women can accomplish. All of us at Liberty Path, including our clients, truly appreciate their support.

"Give thanks in all circumstances; for this is
God's will for you in Christ Jesus"
FIRST THESSALONIANS 5:18

Eat Dessert First!

Patsy, my dearest friend from Northwest Houston BPW, and I met for lunch frequently. One day, we began to question the sanity of waiting until after our meal to eat dessert. "I don't understand why people don't eat dessert first," I said. "After all, if we wait until after we eat our meal, then we're too full."

"You're right. Why don't we order dessert first this time?" asked Patsy. So we did. That's how our Eat Dessert First (EDF) group came to be. Donna, Brenna, Louise, Patsy, and I would meet about once a month. After a time, Janet joined us. Sadly, we haven't gotten together like this since Patsy died. I know she's sad about this as am I. Perhaps we'll start again in her memory. I still like to eat dessert first, and with every bite I think of Patsy, and my heart smiles.

Passion

Do you have a hobby? What is your favorite color? What is your favorite restaurant? For so many years, I didn't have a clue what I liked or didn't like. For years, I was never able to answer when asked these questions. I didn't know who I was, only that I liked music.

"Where do you want to go for dinner?" Randall would ask.

My answer was, "Where ever you want to go is fine with me." So we would go where Randall wanted to go. Then, I would get upset because I didn't really want Chinese food. Then I would pout. Really? How confusing is that?!

A friend of mine suggested I just try different things. Go antique shopping, go to movies, read books, crochet, or learn to knit. Well, I discovered antiques are not my thing. I also discovered crocheting and knitting are relaxing for me. Because I'm somewhat obsessive, I don't knit just one afghan; I knit at least twelve. I don't just crochet one blanket; I crochet one for all my friends. This is not too different from the way I used to drink—all or nothing, but mostly all.

I'm still learning balance. The "all or nothing" mentality is so typical of a recovering alcoholic. When I read, I read an average of five books a week. Just think. I would have finished this book years ago if I had spent as much time writing it as I did reading everyone else's books.

The good news is I now have a voice that can express my desire about what to eat, what to wear, and even my opinions about politics, economics, and the weather. This may be a small thing to you, but to me, it's huge. The voices in my head are silent, and they don't dictate my mind, telling me what I should or shouldn't do. They don't tell me who I am nor who I should be. They no longer tell me lies.

Do you have a voice? Do you know who you are? Do you know what your preferences in food, color, clothes, etc., are? More importantly, can you express them? Yes, you can. God gave us a voice to speak. He gave us a mind to use and a heart to feel. When we use our senses to the fullest and for the purpose of bringing joy to others, what a difference we make not only in our own personal lives, but also—and more importantly—in the lives of others.

"Light in a messenger's eyes
brings joy to the heart, and good news gives health to the bones."
PROVERBS 15:30

Silent Gift

Some people who have lost their sight, hearing, or limbs accomplish great feats in spite of their obvious limitations. I'm always in awe when I read or see how they compensate for their loss by maximizing other gifts God has given them. Being grateful for the gift of deafness—the gift of silence—is my great feat.

My first bout with total deafness came in 2010. At that time, we did not know if it was permanent or not. Over time, my hearing was "on again" and "off again." Randall, my protector and my best friend, immediately set about seeking devices that would aid my functionality. "Look what I found on the Internet: it's a 'Shaker.' You put this device under the mattress, and it will wake you up." He purchased a type of alarm that vibrates under the mattress, so I would know when to get up in the morning because I could no longer hear the alarm.

"How are you going to know when someone comes in the office?" Randall asked. Well, good question. He purchased another device that sends a signal to a receiver I wear. It vibrates when our office door opens so I know someone is there.

Randall also did a lot of research and procured the best phone for me to use in our office, so I can still converse as needed with clients. The phone captions the caller's conversation for me, and it is a lifesaver. Without it, I could not communicate on the phone.

Six weeks into my total hearing loss, my husband took me off-shore fishing, and it was pretty sporty. All of a sudden, as if a wire had connected, I could hear the boat motors. It was wonderful. We were all so thankful, because the restoration of some of my hearing was truly a miracle. The doctors had been wrong; I could still hear enough to function, more than twenty years after their prediction of total deafness.

Unfortunately, in 2011, my hearing left once again and has not yet returned. I still don't know ASL, but that hasn't slowed me down. I praise God for allowing me to practice lip-reading all those years for it has become an invaluable skill. I'm also grateful all the devices necessary for me to function, in addition to my supportive family and friends, and Bailey, our Lab, have made the transition relatively smooth for me.

The most difficult part of my deafness is not the silence; it's the potential for self-pity. Most of the time, I welcome the quiet, which is very peaceful to me. However, I miss not hearing the music at church, and not being able to hear the radio or talk on the phone. Friends send me YouTube links with people talking and songs playing, but most of the time, I am at a loss. Thankfully, some YouTube links do offer closed-captioning. Self-pity is very dangerous for me. It can set me up to drink, so I can't afford to wallow.

God, in His mercy, allows me to hear music—not voices—in my head constantly. I hear the melodies when I look at music. Getting lost in the music when I play the piano is a wonderful escape for me. I feel the music in my mind and in my heart. I get so connected to Chopin, Beethoven, and other great classical composers I forget about being deaf. I hear through my eyes when Bailey barks. The sound of my children's voices are embedded in my brain, so when they speak, I truly hear them.

Forgetful

Can a person forget they are deaf? I do. After all, I was very accustomed to hearing only enough to get by. Sometimes when I open up the Liberty Path office, I see the light on the answering machine blinking, signaling messages have been recorded. I pick up the phone to retrieve the messages, but I can't hear anything. "Hello, Hello! Is anyone there?" Oh, that's right...I can't hear! Thank God for our precious staff who pitch in and surround me with love. They are my ears. Our staff and volunteers are the best. They serve at Liberty Path with hearts for the Lord.

Sometimes, to the frustration of family, friends, and coworkers, I'll ask a question and then turn my back. Because I lip-read, this presents a dilemma for those who are trying to answer me. I truly do forget, and I thank God for their patience with me. This is still pretty new for me. Sometimes, the thought crosses my mind others have adapted better than I have.

Most of the time, the challenges God allows me to experience in my silence are laughable. Sometimes, they are not. Occasionally, anger rears its ugly head. Not long ago, I sent Randall a text that said, "I'm angry that I'm deaf." That was it. Short and sweet.

To be able to text or verbally express my emotion without smashing china, breaking glass, damaging floors, or getting drunk is a big step. This proves God's grace. This proves He still performs miracles each and every day. I'm one of them. I am learning to handle my deafness with a little more grace, and without the bottle as my solution.

Of course, my family, friends, and I are hoping and praying my hearing will be restored, according to His will. However, God has allowed me to live in silence now for several years. Most of the time, this is such a welcome relief from all the years of hearing those horrid, cruel voices battling for my soul. God comforts and reassures through His gift of silence.

"Shout for joy, you heavens; rejoice, you earth;
burst into song, you mountains!
For the Lord comforts his people and will have
compassion on his afflicted ones."
Isaiah 49:13

Silence is...

For the most part, the silence is...well, quiet. Many blessings accompany deafness. For example, our neighbor's dogs bark at three in the morning, but don't present a problem for me. That lawn mower starting up at seven on Saturday morning? No problem. My husband doesn't have to hear any complaining about his snoring. I don't even know if he snores or not. In fact, he tells me that *I'm* the one who snores. I guess he's not deaf.

Would you like a deaf person to counsel you? My deafness *helps* the clients whom I counsel. My clients actually have to look at me and make eye contact. You'd be surprised how many people don't do that. My clients can't look at the floor. Looking at the therapist has been a rewarding challenge for some of our clients. Without realizing it, they are improving their own self-esteem. They are also learning to engage in conversation and to hold their heads up and their shoulders erect, rather than slumped or stooped over.

All new clients at our agency are seen by one of our wonderful therapists, but the ongoing, long-term clients know about my deafness, and I continue to counsel them as needed. They all make an effort to ensure I see what they're saying. Otherwise, I tell them I'll just make it up and it could get interesting.

My clients also can't cover their mouths. Men with facial hair, especially mustaches, and people who have a tendency to mumble present a challenge for me. It takes a tremendous amount of energy for me to focus on what they are saying. By the end of the day, it's not unusual for me to be pretty exhausted from all the concentration, let alone "hearing" about all the pain our clients express from their hearts and minds during counseling sessions. My husband understands this, and is very patient with me. He can see when I've had a tough day. I use my voice and let him know as well, in case there's any doubt. I don't grab a drink, and things don't get broken or smashed anymore, at least not on purpose.

Button Up

Most people don't mind going shopping, whether it's for groceries, clothes, or jewelry. I never enjoyed shopping prior to deafness, and now it's really exhausting, disheartening, and challenging.

I've come to the conclusion maybe there's no pleasure in shopping for me because the cashiers and store clerks typically don't make eye contact when they talk. It also doesn't help nowadays the registers are not always placed where you can see the total of the amount of purchase.

Cashiers are either looking at the cash register or looking through you when they talk. It is very frustrating. At the store, the clerk will ask, "Did you find everything you were looking for?" while looking at their shoes or chewing gum—whatever it takes to *not* look at the customer. It's a rare event when a cashier truly looks at you when speaking to you. Next time, just for grins, when you're at a store, see what happens. You may discover for yourself this is true.

Randall is not the only one who shops online for assistive devices for the hearing impaired or deaf. I purchased some round, colorful buttons with phrases like, "Deaf but Friendly" or "Please face me when speaking. I'm deaf." This doesn't help as often as one would think. Sometimes it helps, but most times it doesn't. Cashiers are not the only ones who avoid looking at you or making eye contact with you when they speak.

Often, someone will come up to me and ask, "What does your pin say?"

If they are looking at me, and I know what they have asked, I reply, "Deaf but friendly."

For some reason, they always respond with pity on their faces and say, "I'm so sorry." I'm not. Maybe a little frustrated though.

My daughter tells me when her friends discover I'm deaf, they start raising their voices. It's funny. If a person is deaf, does it really matter how loud they are spoken to? People's intentions are good. It certainly doesn't bother me, but their loud voices may annoy others. Heather and I often laugh about this.

A few years ago, one of our grandchildren played a part in a musical based on the Broadway play, *Annie.* I went with my husband to show support, but it was one of the most difficult times of silence for me. How I longed to hear those children singing! How I longed to hear the lines they had practiced so hard to perfect. I sat in my silent world, watching others laugh. I tried to fit in with the crowd, as I often do, by laughing when others laughed, applauding when others applauded, and participating to the best of my ability.

Going to concerts is a rare outing for me, although I recognize the value of supporting your friends who perform in local choirs. It's difficult to justify purchasing a ticket for a deaf person, but I go for them. What takes place at these activities is face-time with my friends and family, and above all, time with God. Whether I'm reading His word, worshipping, or praising, I enjoy His presence always.

Whatever activity I attend or wherever I go, it's vital I do not drink. Alcohol was my crutch for so long. Twenty-three years have passed since I had any booze. Alcohol gave me a false sense of courage; it was my companion and my trusted friend. Now, Christ is my friend. I know my Father's grace is sufficient for me, and the Holy Spirit guides me always.

> *"Therefore I will boast all the more gladly about my weaknesses, so that Christ's power may rest on me."*
> SECOND CORINTHIANS *12:9*

What I Thought You Said

My dear friend Patsy and I were visiting one day. What I heard (saw) her say was, "I've got to start studying law." I thought this would be rather challenging. After all, Patsy was in her seventies. Then I remembered Philippians 4:13, which says, "I can do all things through Him who gives me strength." It's never too late to start a new career, right? If anyone could become a lawyer at the age of seventy, it's Patsy. She had authored several books, so a career change now would be in order. I would back her up all the way. That's what friends are for.

What Patsy *really* said was, "I've got to start setting the alarm." Boy, did I get that one wrong.

"Oh, Patsy. I thought you said you were going to start studying law." Studying for a law degree at any age is very challenging, and at our age, it is quite an undertaking. Setting the alarm is easy enough to do. We both laughed until tears streamed down our faces. We needed that laugh. Patsy was battling cancer, and cancer was winning.

Lip-reading takes a lot of practice, and at one time, this gift of mine was in its early stages of development. Because of my pride, I did not make people aware of my disability. Instead, I would pretend to know what they said and, in fact, make up much of the other person's dialogue. I was trying to stay in the context of how I *thought* the conversation was going. This strategy didn't always work.

One time, our family was at the airport, eagerly waiting to leave for a vacation. Our children were still quite young. A gentleman was making casual conversation to pass the time, and asked me, "So, what do you do?"

I thought he asked, "So, how are you?"

I responded, "Very well, thank you. And how are you?" No wonder he looked at me rather quizzically, got up, and moved to another seating section. To this day, Heather and I still laugh about this.

Recently, I was having lunch where my sunshine was working. She came to my table, leaned over closely, and said with a conspirator's look, "I'm going to do the laundry tonight." I thought to myself, *Well, that's nice, dear.* I repeated what I thought she said. After the laughter died down, she wrote on a napkin what she *really* said: "I'm going to win the lottery tonight." Well, I got *some* of the words right. Even with years of practice, I can still get it wrong.

There have been so many other misunderstandings over the years, and the humor has truly provided joy not only to me, but also to my friends and family. It is so wonderful to be able to laugh at myself, and to not take everything so seriously and get my feelings hurt.

Basket of Blessings

Because of God's provision and mercy, our organization celebrated its tenth year of serving Houston at a local church that opened their doors to us. My friend Shannon Perry sang her heart out and also served as our emcee. Our keynote speaker was none other than Mark Lanier, founder of the renowned Lanier Theological Library. Both Shannon and Mark are also authors.

Thanks to the dedication and support of our staff, volunteers, and board of directors, the entire evening was indeed a glorious celebration that honored God for all He has done for and through our ministry. Although the event did not have as many as expected in attendance, the harvest was plentiful.

Through God's grace, we hope to continue to provide counseling to all in need of our services. Why? You may not see through someone's smile the brokenness of his or her heart. Unlike most physical disabilities, emotional scars from trauma, abuse, and addictions are not always visible. We want to help heal the unseen wounds. We want to walk with the young children full of anger and confusion, leading them on a brighter path. We want to be an extension of God's grace and help draw others closer to Him. After all, He is the path to liberty and the light that guides us along the way.

This is the message we have heard from him and declare to you:
God is light; in him there is no darkness at all.
First John 1:5

CONCLUSION

HAS SHARING MY journey openly with you given you hope through the tears, the pain, and the laughter? Have you experienced similar pain in your life? You, too, can heal. It is possible because nothing is too great for our Creator.

There are recovery and support groups, counseling centers, and peers that can offer therapy, understanding, and encouragement, in the event you do not have a supportive family. Just remember you are not alone! God never left me, and He will never leave you. He will be there for you, too. He loves you just as you are. He will put people in your life to help guide you on your journey. Please rejoice with me in my recovery from abuse and alcoholism. I am totally healed from past afflictions, and have fully recovered from my addictions thanks to Him.

If you want to heal as I have done, get any professional help that is needed. Take care of your physical body, too, which is God's temple, according to 1 Corinthians 6:19.

Finally, I urge you to accept Christ as Lord of your life. Surrender your afflictions, your addictions, your past, your future, and your pain to His care. He can take it from you. Accept Christ as your Lord and Savior and ask Him to come into your heart. It's that simple. He can remove the voices of evil lies. He can soothe your troubled mind. He can give you His comfort in whatever area you need.

Sobering Thoughts and Reflections

I encourage therapists to take heed to the following summary: "Alcohol abuse can cause signs and symptoms of depression, anxiety, psychosis, and antisocial behavior. At times, these alcohol-related conditions usually disappear after several days or weeks of abstinence. Prematurely labeling these conditions as major depression, panic disorder, schizophrenia, psychosis, or anti-social personality disorder can lead to misdiagnosis." (http://pubs.niaaa.nih.gov/publications/arh26-2/90-98.htm.)

My Heart / His Word

Women and men of all ages who have elected to give up their child for adoption have received counseling at our center. These precious individuals made a beautiful sacrifice so their child could have a better life. God understands and honors their sacrifice. He promises to make not just *some* things right, but *all* things right. (Romans 8:28) Adoption procedures have greatly improved since the early 1950s and most adoptive parents today are loving, caring, and nurturing. Adoption is a beautiful gift not only to your child, but to yourself, because it is God who will work all things out for His glory.

Surfing and Literature

Some key words to put in your search engines for information you may find useful are as follows:
Childhood Trauma
Mental Health
Suicide Prevention
Sexual Abuse Recovery
Substance Abuse
Support Groups

Alcoholism
Drug Addiction
Recovery
Bible Scriptures

If you would like to check out the Twelve Steps of Recovery together with scriptural references, I suggest the following website: www.alcoholicsvictorious.org.

The following books are, in my humble opinion, required reading for anyone who wishes to recover: *The Holy Bible* and *Alcoholics Anonymous*

What's Next?

As a direct result of the path God has allowed me to take, and through His grace, I have developed a methodology we use at our counseling center. This methodology provides tools that can help expedite our clients' road to recovery. It is my heart's desire that one of my future publications will make this methodology available for you.

Thank you for going with me on this journey. I would love to hear from you, so please email me at Dr.V@erikovalk.com. If you're in the Houston area, let's get together!

"For God so loved the world that he gave his one and only Son,
that whoever believes in him shall not
perish but have eternal life"
Jᴏʜɴ *3:16*

Author's Bio

Eriko N. Valk, phd, known by her friends and peers as "Dr. V" is the founder of Liberty Path, Inc., a Christian-based nonprofit counseling center where she, together with other therapists, have helped people recover since 2004.

In 2009 a local television station (KPRC) and a local Christian radio station (KSBJ) awarded Eriko the prestigious Jefferson Award after one of her clients nominated her. Eriko was also elected to represent NW Houston Business and Professional Women as their Woman of Excellence during the same year. She speaks at area churches and has made several television appearances.

Eriko possesses doctoral degrees in social work and psychology and has channeled her education and experience for the sole purpose of helping others heal.

Through God's grace, Eriko overcame abuse, abandonment, and addiction. She has been leading a sober life since 1991.

Eriko and her husband Randall live in Houston, Texas, together with their yellow lab who rules.